Yeller Dawgs--

Texans Who Can't Vote Republican in 2016

third edition

Hal Reames

Acknowledgements

My thanks to the men and women who talked to me about their values and their concerns for our nation. Some took their time to speak with the recorder running. A few sent me their thoughts in writing. Others tolerated my presence at their meetings, knowing that I was taking notes.

As always, I thank my wife--fellow writer and fellow psychologist, Ana Cecilia Carvalho--for her encouragement, her tolerance for political conversations which interest her very little, and for her editorial help.

Finally, I thank Wikimedia for giving free access to the photos that appear on the cover.

Table of Contents

INTRODUCTION

This book reports on interviews with a group of Texans who differ in opinion on a variety of political issues but have one thing in common: None of them will vote Republican in 2016. Most of the interview subjects were encountered at meetings of an informal group that calls itself the Yeller Dawgs. "Yeller Dawg Democrat" is a term came from a South which voted Democratic from the time of Lincoln to the Civil Rights legislation of the 1960's. After Lincoln, they used to say, "I'd vote for an ol' yeller dog before I'd vote for a Republican," but not so often these days. After signing one of the civil rights bills, LBJ reportedly said, "Now we've lost the South for the next thirty years." One might guess that race relations had something to do with Lyndon's prediction.

The identity of the group, itself, is not hard to uncover; and the real names of its members are not secret. They trustingly told me their views and how they came to possess them; but the spouse of one member objected to including information which might be embarrassing to family members. This made perfect sense to me, so the names of all the interviewees have been altered. I have also altered some identifying information and left out many details to provide each speaker with a degree of deniability.

There was one exception to this approach, my posthumous "interview" with deceased playwright, Horton Foote, a Texas native. This interview is set off in an Appendix because some readers might consider it fictional.

The result of these interviews may come as no news to a registered Democrat and will likely be considered as anathema by my Republican friends, relatives, and fellow countrymen. As my target audience, that leaves a few curious Republicans, every Independents and folks who might not otherwise vote in this pivotal election.

I attended my first Yeller Dawg meeting in the summer of 2015. By then, they'd been meeting every Saturday for almost forty years, with two exceptions: First, they never meet if Christmas were to fall on a Saturday; second, they failed to meet one other time, but no one would explain why.

The first person I met after moving from Michigan to Texas in 2005 would try to dispute LBJ's view of the South as a bastion of racism. At my first meeting with the Yeller Dawgs, I introduced myself with this true story:

I backed the UHaul into my new driveway in Bastrop and went inside to view the new digs before unloading every worldly possession I hadn't heaved into the dumpster back in Michigan. I had barely closed the bathroom door when a knock came at the front.

"Hi, neighbor," said a lady several years my junior and apparently in moderate distress. Before I could say "Hi," or "I'm sorry if I ran over your cat," she said, "I see from your license plate that you're from up North. I just want you to know that the Civil War wasn't about slavery."

A number of thoughts ricocheted through my road-weary brain: "What do you think was the purpose of States' Rights if not to protect the institution of slavery? What else lay at the heart of the Missouri Compromise?" As well as, "What is your name, Neighbor Lady?"

(This southern belief about the Civil War was examined by the 6/22/15 issue of <u>The Atlantic</u>, in an article by Ta-Neshi Coates titled, "What this Cruel War was Over." The following document was claimed to be Mississippi's explanation for secession:

"Our position is thoroughly identified with the institution of slavery—the greatest material interest of the world. Its labor supplies the product which constitutes by far the largest and most important portions of commerce of the earth. These products are peculiar to the climate verging on the tropical regions, and by an imperious law of nature, none but the black race can bear exposure to the tropical sun. These products have become necessities of the world, and a blow at slavery is a blow at commerce and civilization. That blow has been long aimed at the institution, and was at the point of reaching its consummation. There was no choice left us but submission to the mandates of abolition, or a dissolution of the Union, whose principles had been subverted to work out our ruin..."

In addition, Carl T. Bogus wrote an article for the University of California in which he argued that Virginia refused to join the revolution without a Second Amendment because Virginians like Jefferson feared a slave revolt.[1])

But I couldn't have read either article back in 2005, so instead I just told her, "Hi."

---

[1] Law Review (1998), 309, arguing that the right to bear arms in "organized militia" referred to the fact that "The Georgia statutes required patrols, under the direction of commissioned militia officers, to examine every plantation each month and authorized them to search 'all Negro Houses for offensive Weapons and Ammunition' and to apprehend and give twenty lashes to any slave found outside plantation grounds"
http://www.truth-out.org/news/item/13890-the-second-amendment-was-ratified-to-preserve-slavery

Before I sat back down at this meeting of the Yeller Dawgs, I voiced my quandary: "You're southern folks but can't seem to vote Republican like most of your brethren, and I wonder why not."

They didn't jump to their feet to address my implication that the South's newfound Republicanism had fulfilled President Johnson's race-based prediction. In fact, they didn't respond at all, so I decided to take my questions to them one at at time.

Anybody with a FaceBook page has heard rants from all over the political spectrum. The interviews which follow contain some of such rants, but the point of the interviews is to demonstrate that the opinions of the Yeller Dawgs are based on the life experiences of thoughtful people.

Chapter 1: Son of a Farmer

First, I took my question to a private meeting with Woodrow, a ninety-six years old professor emeritus who'd been one of the founders of the group almost forty years ago. After hearing a brief telling of this erudite economist's story, a thoughtful reader will not be able to dismiss it out of hand. Considering all of the events he has witnessed in his long life and his knowledge of economic systems, we ignore his warnings at our own peril.

First called the "Saturday Sages," the group started one day when he and a State Senator met over coffee to talk politics. They enjoyed it so much they decided to meet regularly. Right away, they included a local bookstore owner (Half-Priced Books), and the three--reminiscent of the "three philosophers" who famously met at Austin's Barton Springs--soon attracted others.

Woodrow, the last surviving founder, moderated the conversations for their first thirty-years, during which the group has never acquired any formal structure, no officers, no dues, no rules. After he turned the gavel over to a man named Mack, the group adopted its current moniker, "The Yeller Dawgs."

At my first meeting Yeller Dawg meeting, Mack, a youthful 89, nodded to Woodrow. The economist rose, stood tall above the front table, and addressed the group clearly and solemnly. He argued that the world appeared to be headed toward a recession and didn't think the U.S. economy, with its much-reduced industrial capability, had the strength to pull the rest of the world out of a recession.

His mastery of information impressed me, but I did feel some concern about his face. He appeared to be wearing a purple battle mask which covered his forehead and had a span which reached down between his eyes and then spread to cover the rest of his face except his nose.

"I bumped into a door," he explained to the assembled.

I'd heard such explanations from battered women, but Woodrow had been living in the same retirement home for many years, alone now that his wife had passed away, and he didn't seem like a man who'd countenance mistreatment. He was, however, willing to tolerate my questions, and we arranged a meeting.

After I found my way to Woodrow's building in the massive retirement and nursing-care complex, he guided me to a little alcove where we could talk without any resident traffic. Here I would undertake my first interview with an actual Yeller Dawg, though he preferred the name, "Saturday Sage" and smiled ironically when he said it.

First, he asked, "How much time do you need? I have to go back to my room and put my feet up by 1:00. My kidneys aren't working at full strength, so my legs swell. I have to wear these rubber stockings," which he showed me, "and there is always a risk of clotting." He then explained that he takes blood thinners, but they made him "bleed like a stuck pig." That explained the purple face, now cleared up.

After a distinguished academic career, a retirement that has lasted almost as long, and the loss of his wife, Woodrow must now fight a constant battle against the health problems that result from spending so many years on the planet. Not exactly youthful, myself, I silently doubted I'd be tolerating interviews if I reached ninety-six.

His body was failing him. He'd lost his wife. But he did not stop trying to teach people the limitations of the economic system he knew so well, both as a professor of economics and a child of the depression.

Woodrow originally haled from Westminster, Texas, an unincorporated community that lies northeast of Dallas and currently boasts a population of 861. It was a cotton-growing area before 1929 but lost access to the railroad in the Great Depression and dwindled to a population of 268. When the Depression hit, Woodrow had just finished high school. He didn't describe an easy life, even before the crash.

Explaining the area, Woodrow said that after the abolition of slavery, three ethnic groups at the bottom of the economic scale competed for jobs and tenancy on farmland--poor whites, freed slaves and their descendants, and ethnic Mexicans. Even during the 1920's White job seekers were putting up signs that read, "Leave or Die." According to Woodrow, these were intended more for Mexican tenant farmers than Blacks, but other signs would say, "Nigger, get out of town by sunset."

"Towns that would lynch any Black person found in town after dark were called 'Sunset towns,' and people took pride in that attitude," he told without any editorial comment.

Clearly remembering my introductory comments about my neighbor's denial of southern racism, Woodrow told the story how a black family's car broke down at sunset one Christmas Eve. The car contained a man, his pregnant wife, and their two children. Rather than lynch the man and his pregnant wife and then figure out what to do with their two children on Christmas morning, the mayor helped them get their car fixed and on their way out of town. This was the humane exception that proved the rule, a generous act of decency committed in the context of a murderous system.

Winning the right to work as a tenant farmers in the 1920's apparently just led to perpetual servitude. Even before the Great Depression hit, the system kept them borrowing the money needed to farm and to survive but never earning enough from crops to pay off the debt.

Woodrow was expected to help in the fields as a child, but "for a number of reasons" he had trouble. One reason, he explained, was that "the dust covered my face and glasses and ran into my eyes" as he sweat in the heat.

Those glasses resulted from what I imagine was one of Woodrow's rare acts of disobedience at school. He had found a penknife on the school grounds, and his observant teacher caught him with it, thought the little delinquent needed closer supervision, and moved him to the front row to keep an eye on him. She soon found that she had a very bright student on her hands because Woodrow could now read what she was writing on the blackboard.

That illicit penknife changed Woodrow's life. He soon received his first pair of glasses, which gave him and his parents the vision to open one door and close another. The newly bespectacled tenant-farmer's son was looking more and more like college material at the same time that his glasses, muddied by sweat and dust, interfered with farm work. The torture of farm work would end if somehow his family could send him to college.

Before Roosevelt had started the New Deal, this tenant farmer's son was facing a grim future of stinging eyes and endless debt. The New Deal didn't come in time to save him from the economic conditions, but education would. "Somehow the family scraped together a few hundred dollars" to send him to college. There, he would save money by living with a cousin.

Once Woodrow started college, he stayed in Austin for summer school rather than return to the fields. After a couple of years, he'd taken so many economics courses, he became a teaching assistant and could pay his own way for the rest of his undergraduate education.

"Free enterprise" wasn't working well for the small farmer in Texas before and during the depression. Informed by this experience with "unregulated capitalism," Woodrow concluded, "Capitalism is such a reckless thing left to itself that there has to be regulation. Only then will it succeed. We'd have enough government regulation if we had the right kind. Currently it's often regulated by the wrong people and for the wrong purposes.[2] We'd do well to develop a sort of

---

[2] He said, "There's an interesting article by Paul Krugman today about how much of the regulation that the government has done is to benefit the oil industry. We have the problem that they are too powerful to control."

welfare state along the European model, a mixed economy, but the only way change happens is through adaptation of the old system into something somewhat different."

Woodrow had experienced first-hand how the unrestrained free market led to competition between countrymen, deadly competition leading not just to lowered wages, but violence and discrimination. He knew in his heart, in a way the man who grew up wealthy can't know, that guided only by the profit-motive, free markets alone can't allocate resources to societal needs and could never have forged the country into a unified, slave-free nation. And Woodrow didn't learn it from some textbook. He learned it by watching his family struggle in a quicksand of tenant farming, borrowing more each year for the next crop, watching as a little boy through eyes stinging with sweat and dust.

By the age of twenty he had "picked up a couple of degrees" from the University of Texas. Woodrow was teaching there in 1941 when Pearl Harbor was attacked. Then he joined the Air Corps; and during the occupation of Japan, he taught economics at the University of Tokyo. After four years in Air Corps, the World War II vet got a Masters and then a Ph.D. from Columbia. He had faculty jobs at Tufts, University of California, as well as a decade at Cal. Berkeley. He also taught at Buffalo and then came back to U.T. from 1960 until 1986 when he retired as a full professor.

This distinguished sage, who has witnessed a century of U.S. history, who has studied under the nation's foremost economists, who has taught economics all over the world, has this clear advice for us in this, an election year:

He recommended neither unrestrained capitalism nor government ownership of the business sector. He thought the U.S. would be better served by regulated capitalism like that found northern Europe. "Whatever we can construct must evolve from what currently exists," he cautioned. "Economic forces need guidance and regulation by policymakers."

In answer to my question about various candidates' talk of instituting tariffs to protect U.S. businesses, he said, "Tariffs are a primitive tool in international economy. We need trade agreements. The US is not going back to factories, not as long Asians will do factory work for a fraction. We have to continue in the direction Clinton set with NAFTA and our deindustrialization."

He also voiced doubts that Bernie Sanders would be able to bring about a "political revolution" but thought "his and Senator Elizabeth Warren's influence [is] good. And I see both of them as a modern version of new Dealers [befitting] the current situation."

These warnings and advice come from a non-politician, a capitalist economist, a man who grew up working a farm in the Texas dust, a man who needs to amass no wealth, a man with no philosophical axe to grind, a man who thinks clearly in his ninety-sixth year.

Chapter 2: The Investment Advisor

After the interview process had nearly reached its end, the Yeller Dawgs were discussing of the Supreme Court's ruling in the Citizen's United case when Cal stood up. He looked familiar, but I hadn't seen him at many meetings so I had no idea what he might say. His interview is included early in this report because it illustrates what Woodrow had to say about the recklessness of unrestrained capitalism.

"Bernie Sanders is saying that the big banks have to be broken up, that Glass-Steagall has to be resurrected. Well, I work for a Wall Street firm. I am a stockbroker and am nearing retirement. I have spent my professional life helping people invest and build their retirement and financial security for their families, and I can tell you about Wall Street."

These words sucked the air out of the room. And he'd just started:

"It is absolutely true! Beginning in the spring of 1987, the brokerage houses changed. The reps they sent out from Wall Street had a totally different agenda. They pressured us to sell all kinds of risky derivatives. When I pointed out that these 'investments' could collapse, they said, 'They're bulletproof,' *bullet proof,* meaning, 'We make money if they go up, but we also make money if they go down. We can't get hurt either way.' (*We* meant the brokers, not the investors.)

"I never sold any of that junk to my clients. That's not why I became an investment advisor. I did it to help people plan for the future, not to make the most money possible for myself. The movies you're seeing and stories you're hearing about Wall Street's greed are absolutely true now!"

I approached Cal as soon as the meeting broke up, and we arranged a meeting at the Magnolia Cafe on South Congress. When the date arrived, I lay my recorder between his beer and my coffee and pressed "record":

Cal explained that he was just "finishing up" his career and planned to retire in mid-summer. I told him what I was writing, and he said he could contribute an understanding of the "poisoning of our economic system so it is no longer free enterprise. It's rampant, unbridled capitalism."

I found that an interesting distinction. He went on: "It's almost to the point now where money talks and everything else walks. The rich and powerful get more rich and powerful. And many of those people are on Wall Street. I've seen the complexion of Wall Street change in just the short time I've been there.

"I'm just a ham and eggs investment advisor. I'm not a big guy out on Wall Street making one or two million dollars. I'm not a little guy either. I'm sort of in the middle in terms of asset management, but I've see a lot. I have a lot of experience, and I've taken good notes, and I've seen not only Wall Street but... our whole society undergo a transformation to the point that hard work and democracy are no longer considered virtues. Now, the most virtuous person is some son-of-a-bitch who has the most money, regardless of how he gets it. And that's particularly true on Wall Street. You're rewarded on Wall Street, not so much for making the right investment decisions (for your clients) but for putting a lot of money under management, and to do that you focus on higher net-worth clients.

As the years go by, you lose your focus and you lose your empathy for people who are just starting their lives and trying to build wealth. It's no longer about the helping teacher with financial planning so she can put her kids through school. They don't care about those people any more. They care about the higher net-worth people.

But *I* come from a family of teachers. My parents were teachers, and I came from a middle class background. We never had any money. In my early years on Wall Street as an investment broker, I helped teachers. I helped blue-collar people, oil field workers. I helped plumbers. I helped a lot of people just starting out trying to build wealth. Along the way, I got pretty damn good at what I did. I read all the time and learned how to work the stock market, how to invest, and I also acquired more and more net-worth clients as the twenty-nine years progressed.

During that time, two things disillusioned me the most: (1), the prevalence of arrogance on the Street, not giving a damn about helping lower and middle income people develop wealth, and (2), what they could get away with by financially engineering poisonous products."

"The recession in 2008 wasn't an accident?" I asked innocently.

"It was engineered. The mechanism they used to create these financially engineered products rose from the ashes of the Glass-Steagall act (of 1933) being repealed in December of 1999. And in the spring of I think it was 2000, the CFTC (Commodity Futures Trading Commission) regulations were watered down to basically nothing. (Wendy Graham, Phil Graham's wife, sat on the board of the CFTC. She was also on the Board of Enron.) So once you do away with that structure of regulation and oversight, the barn door is open, and they all scattered out to seek their fortunes by taking advantage of there being no cops on the street. If you had the biggest, fastest hot rod, you could race and didn't have to worry about getting a ticket, and that's what happened. You could speed all you wanted.

"The foundation for the housing crisis that started to present itself in the summer of '07 was actually being laid by 2001 and 2002, early in the Bush years. And as the months and the years rolled by, they got braver and braver, more arrogant, more bulletproof, to the point that they said, "We can do any damn thing we want."

"So what did they do? They engineered products that were derivatives based on [the belief in] an ever-expanding housing industry in our country. Since World War II, housing prices had never gone down--never, though isolated pockets of weakness appeared from time to time. The sand states--Arizona, California, Nevada, Florida--in those four states in particular, housing was moving. And so if you were going to bet on the ever-rising housing market, there were four or five different ways to do it on Wall Street. It became more and more sophisticated: From loan origination, loan processing, and loan securitization, to lack of regulation on all of the above, to outright fraud in the pooling of the mortgages, and outright fraud by those who insured those mortgages, and it all worked perfectly for awhile.

"When Uncle Joe and Aunt Polly, who were school teachers and had salaries totalling $120,000 per year, went to buy a house worth $600-700,000, which they could not afford, they went to a loan officer, who now said, "Sure, you can qualify! No problem."

"So they go look at the house, and ask, 'Can we afford this house? It's got a pool. It's a six thousand square foot home.'

"'Sure, we'll show you how to do it.'

"So the first flaw was inadequate loan documentation and due diligence. Instead of saying 'No' to the mortgage they said, 'Buy the damn house! If you lose your job and can't make the mortgage payments, sell it because the value's going to keep going up.'

"So, do the math. The mortgage payments on that house are six or seven times more than they can afford. But the loan officer wants his commission for selling the home. Uncle Joe and Aunt Polly buy the house with a bare minimum down payment or maybe none at all."

Then Cal delivered a mini lecture on the instruments involved in the housing collapse. He described levels of these "poison products."

(Those who don't want to hear the details should skip ahead:)

After you do hundreds of thousands or millions mortgages like this, the banks say, "We can make money another way on these loans. We'll pool them together worth maybe $500,000,000 and we'll issue bonds against this pool. You buy the bond, and we'll give you an accelerated interest rate, and as they are paid off, you'll receive a return of principal gradually but you'll receive an interest rate constantly."

"What's my risk?" asks the investor.

"No problem! You've got a big, diversified loan portfolio. If ten per cent go broke, you've got 90% paying on their mortgages. No problem!"

That is engineered product #1.

Now, you put pools of mortgages together and a bank sells 400,000 mortgages to J.P. Morgan Bank in New York and gets a big commission. The big bank that buys these mortgages gets a commission to underwrite them, to put them in a pool of mortgages and underwrite the securities against that pool. That's leverage # 2.

Leverage #3 says, "Hey, we know another way to make money on this. Let's create something called a credit default swap, which protects the bank that owns this pool of mortgages if defaults start to occur. So they create another security, and the banks get another fee for underwriting those securities. A credit default swap goes up in value as failures and delinquencies go down.

But who's gonna secure the credit default swaps? Let's get a giant insurance company. Which one could handle this? Lords of London won't do it. Hey, AIG! They sell an insurance policy and receive a premium. Everybody's happy. That's #4.

Leverage #5: A collateralized debt obligation. It is a bond issued against a pool of mortgages. We are going to package these pools of mortgages in a way that overinflates their value and looks good, maybe better than it really is. How? They go to the great neighborhoods with high net-worth mortgages and package those mortgages. But they don't have enough of those, so they gather middle and lower-class folks' mortgages, but they still don't have enough. Then they go to sub-prime mortgages, which were about 15% of mortgages sold in this country back then. They are people who have nothing and include lots of minorities. They are sold with the same pitch: "Sell it if you lose your job." (And that is the belief: The US housing market has not gone down since World War II, and it won't now.)

The major Wall Street firms that packaged these pools of mortgages don't have enough of the good quality types so they put them in the pool with the bad quality and middle quality mortgages and sold it to AIG, other banks, or some other financial institution. Many pools of mortgages were poisoned by subprime mortgages.

"Some of these mortgage people would come down from New York or from Houston, before crash and tell us, 'It's perfectly safe. It can't go down... great investments for your clients.' That was one of the things that got my attention about 2005 or 6. I'd ask them, 'What is this and tell me how it works in one sentence?' They couldn't do it, and I smelled a rat. I'm not the only one, so we didn't do that. Guys at the top asked why we wouldn't, but generally they left us alone and just kept giving us incentives. Those who did take the bait and were fired or left after the crash just walked across the street to another firm. I started getting disillusioned, and it's grown more and more pronounced as years go by.

"But the poison didn't start to take effect until something else happened in early spring of '07. A guy by the name of John Paulson, a hedge fund manager, was flying over Arizona on the way to the west coast, and he looked down and saw all these brown matchsticks, (the wooden frames of all the houses being built), and he thought, "This has to be the peak of the housing market. With all of this housing, home prices cannot keep going up." He forecast a decline and started shorting, and he sold some of those shorts to his buddies at Goldman Sachs, betting that they were going to go down in value and he was going to make a lot of money. And Goldman Sachs took his side of the bet and made a lot of money.[3] The losers were those who ended up holding the paper. That's when it started to crumble, in the fall and late summer of '07.

Meanwhile, time was catching up with middle-income workers. Their jobs were being shipped overseas to cheaper labor markets, and layoffs started to happen. When Uncle Joe lost his factory job, Aunt Polly went to work. When she lost her job, they had only one thing left that they could to do to make up for that lost income: They could borrow against the mortgage.

When the mortgage defaults grew, AIG couldn't honor the insurance policies and went broke. The banks went broke because had too much of this stuff on their balance sheets. The housing market kept deteriorating. People kept getting laid off."

Question: What would the Wall Street guys say when you pointed out that Polly and Joe have lost their savings for retirement?

"I don't care. I'm making money."

Question: "How did repealing Glass-Steagall make this happen?"

---

[3] For normal people who aren't familiar with selling "short," it's done when a trader expects the value of what he is trading to go down. He/she always wants to buy low and sell high, and that's what he's doing, except he's selling first at the high price and buying later after the price has dropped. Since transactions aren't finalized until the end of the trading day, he can buy later than he sold and fill his earlier sell order with his later purchase.

"Repealing Glass-Steagall was a tragic mistake because it removed the wall between investment banking and commercial banking." Seeing my blank stare, Cal went on: "Because if a small company wants to get operating capital (under Glass-Steagall), they used to go to a bank and get a loan. Without Glass-Steagall in place, the bank says, "We have an investment banking arm. Go to them. They'll take you public.""

What's wrong with that? I'm thinking.

Cal looks into my glassy eyes and says, "The investment arm of the bank goes to their customers and talks up the stock. The analyst will sell a lot, thereby inflating the stock price, get his fee, and then the head of the company is on his own with the capital he needed.

"That was going on in the late 1920's. Glass-Steagall prevented that crap. The law was their for a reason. Republicans were getting campaign money from big banks and were pushing for its repeal. Bill Clinton was getting money from Sandy Wyle, the CEO of Citigroup. He told Clinton, 'Break down this barrier. We have great intentions... and deep pockets... the economy is good.' Phil Gramm kept warning of recession and needing to stimulate the economy, but it wasn't true. We had a great stock market, but Clinton went along with it. In December of '99, it passed both houses, and he signed it.

"So they deregulated banks and commodity futures, and 63,000 factories shut down between '86 and 2000, something like that. Jobs were exported, and that can only go on so long before the middle class starts to feel it. You might Google that number.[4]

"Nineteen ninety-nine, that's when the first nail hit the coffin. When there are no more cops on the street, drivers get more aggressive, more arrogant.

Question: "So, Texan, why aren't you voting Republican in 2016?"

"Republicans are financed by the wealthy--Wall Street, insurance companies, oil. It's the party of the wealthy. Democrats are party of middle class and opportunity for all, to lift all boats. Republicans only care about the big boats."

Question: "What kind of candidate inspires your trust?"

"I absolutely adore Bernie Sanders. He smelled those rats early. I think he was one(of only eight Senators who voted against the Glass-Steagall repeal in '99. Banks are bigger and stronger and more influential than ever before. Two hundred-ten billion in fines were assessed against the banking industry for mortgage fraud, mortgage packaging fraud, and securities fraud. They've paid and are continuing to pay them. Fees were negotiated down through the legal

---

[4] Googling, I didn't find that figure, but I did learn that 42,000 factory jobs have been lost since 2000. http://prospect.org/article/plight-american-manufacturing

system. But the five major Wall Street banks have more assets now than ever. They have cash of about two and a half-trillion dollars.[5]

---

[5] Parenthetically I asked: Does that mean you are a Sanders supporter?

"Practically speaking, I don't think breaking up the banks is the thing to do. I'm for taking a more pragmatic approach, and that is why I support Hillary. She wants to look at the big picture, not just the banks, but the insurance companies, the whole financial industry, and enforce Dodd-Frank (the Wall Street Reform and Consumer Protection Act), tweak Dodd-Frank. She has not come out and said anything about renewing Glass-Steagall, but I do think that you can't plan for the future by looking through the rear view mirror. Maybe the banks don't need to be broken up, but maybe they do need more regulation. Or, maybe they *do* need to be broken up. It's a debate worth having.

With Bernie as president he'd have the hopeless task of fighting with the Republicans to get anything done. He may be ineffective. I don't think it's in the cards for the Democrats to win the Senate, so he would have to compromise too much. We can make some structural changes that are substantial and meaningful and that can help the banking industry.

I think Hillary's in a position to really get something done for us with her background. I'm for going in with a surgical scalpel instead of a hatchet. Bernie's dead on, but he can't get it done.

Chapter 3: A Man Opposed to the "Racket"

Mack, the current moderator of the Yeller Dawg meetings, had invited me to the first meeting. He provided the most detailed interview, and I typed up more than fifty pages for his family archives. His entire life story is relevant to his eventual politics, but the following shortened version is included to provide the reader with a portrait of a man who reached his convictions after almost ninety years of the American experience. A remarkably intelligent man, a working man, a family man, a man who has always made up his own mind, Mack has always learned from personal experience and has taken nothing on blind faith. Carl's expert testimony regarding Wall Street was presented first to demonstrate the most recent example of what Mack calls the "racket."

I was standing outside a restaurant, waiting for Mack when the Yeller Dawgs started to assemble. "Here he comes," said a welcoming Yeller Dawg named Cole.

At that point, a big sedan coasted across the parking lot and onto the sidewalk, practically entering the restaurant through the front door. It stopped in time, then withdrew to the asphalt, and a smiling, energetic man popped out. "I'm going to have to quit driving when my license comes up for renewal. With my macular degeneration, I'm practically blind," he said with a chuckle.

"Are you Mack?" I asked, introducing myself.

Mack had taken over running the meetings a few years before I arrived at the Yeller Dawg doorstep. Though a very different man than Professor Woodrow, and just seven years younger than his predecessor, Mack too got a good look at the Depression, and it shaped his opinions regarding unrestrained capitalism and the politicians who supported it. Officially speaking, Mack is not an educated man. He has no college degree, after all. His resume, if he wrote one, would first list him as a printer, then as the owner of a printing shop; and in the early years of computers, before the popularity of the desktop computer, it would describe him as the proprietor of a business where people could rent computer time. Such a sketchy resume would not explain why he, unlike many Texans with a trade and a small business, couldn't vote Republican. In Mack's own words:

My father read water meters. He walked that entire town of Corsicana, [population, twenty thousand] once a month, read the meters, repaired the meters, replaced the meters, and partially calculated the bills. He figured the total water consumption so that other people would translate it into dollars... [Money was tight] and so my two older brothers and my sister and I--I was the youngest--all had jobs from the very beginning, tending the garden and bringing in the eggs. We kept chickens in town at that time.

I started helping my oldest brother deliver papers. I would take one side of the street and he would take the big bundle on the other side. And then, you know, I had my own paper route by the time I was ten; and then at thirteen, I got a job in a printing company. At first I'd just run and get cokes and sweep out, that sort of thing. In February of 1940, I guess it was, I was thirteen, and this was the largest printing company in Corsicana. There were three others...

In November of that year--I believe it was November 25--they mobilized the National Guard. My recollection is that there were two printers, the two men in the back shop. They got notice on Thursday to show up at 6 a.m. on Monday and ship out. At thirteen I was suddenly "the Man" because the owner was an excellent typesetter and could spell anything and knew the music composers better than the music teachers and knew how to spell Tchaikovsky four different ways, all of them accurate. But he was totally at a loss mechanically. You'd ask him to hand you the pliers and you might get a hammer or a screwdriver or any damn thing.

I had a key to come in and clean up on the weekends and whatnot, and I was fascinated with this equipment and had learned to run all of it on my own just by watching. I had started using it to print myself some little business cards, some little dance programs for high school, you know, just for our group that was having little private dances. Knowing how to run the equipment, I was suddenly a valuable employee. I went from $.50 a week to $7.00 a week.

I only lived about four blocks from the shop. I went to school in the morning, and put up whatever jobs the boss had left me. I'd get them set up for approval, and he and his niece would run them; but if anything went wrong, they were up shit creek, so to speak. Then I'd run home and run on to school which was another five blocks; and then at lunch, I would beat it down to that printing shop to find out what they needed. I'd set up another job, or I'd fix whatever'd happened."

At this point in his life, Mack experienced an epiphany that led him to call himself a socialist, but it mustn't be told until his entire working life has been briefly summarized. After that point, the story will flash back to this job.

I was having trouble with my dad mainly. My mom was more considerate of my opinion. My dad wanted me "stay in school" and to "quit that damn gettin up early and goin down to that printing company" and this and that, and he wanted me to bring books home. Hell, I'd never brought books home. I'd throw 'em in my locker.

In May of 1942 I was fifteen and had a fallin out with my dad. I'd gotten too big for my britches, and I left on my thumb, never intending to go back to live; and I was fortunate enough to get picked up by the mayor of the little town fifteen miles east on the way to Tyler.

I was kind of a rebel. I thought I was, back before the '60's. I was smokin and probably had my foot up on the dash and had my shirt unbuttoned probably to my navel. And he says, "Where you goin'?"

And I say, "Tyler."

"Oh, whatcha doin there?"

"Job."

"Oh, what do you do?"

"Printer."

And he says, "I was talkin to the feller who runs the newspaper there. I'm the mayor of Currant. That's as far as I'm goin. It's just fifteen miles. He was tellin me he's lookin for a printer."

"Oh?"

"If you like, I'll take you over there and introduce you. It's just two blocks off the highway, so if you fellas don't make a deal, you know, you can just get back on the highway."

So, sure enough, I walked into this place, this big, old building with really old equipment, and the floors creaked and whatnot. And this guy, Ed, was on the phone and reared back, with his foot on the desk, and he gave us a "Come on in! Have a seat!" He was talkin and laughin, and I liked him right off. So, sure enough, we made a deal pretty quick; and then his wife come in, and I liked her right off too. She was a pretty lady about thirty and she'd been wantin kids for a couple of years but they were unable to, and they both kind of latched onto me. So I got a job for $9 a week, a room, and one meal a day.

I liked the work and we liked each other, and everything went well, and she started introducing me as their adopted son pretty quick. And that was rewarding, personally. I settled down a lot. I had a lot of respect for them. I even buttoned my shirt. When September came, I wasn't expecting to go back to school.

And they said, "You got to go to school,"

And I said, "Oh, no, been there. Done that."

And Ed said, "I'm on the school board. I can't have any truant working for me. You gotta leave or go to school."

So he set it up so I could go to school in the mornin--I only had three courses--and work for him in the afternoon. I'd go to school Monday, Tuesday, and Wednesday and work in the afternoon for him, and we'd work all afternoon and all night Wednesday getting the newspaper out. In those days we didn't have any spare parts. If something broke down you had to fix it yourself. The only help you could get was maybe an electrician or a blacksmith. If a linotype broke, you had to get that part welded.

I'd work all night on Wednesday night till 2:00 Thursday afternoon and skip school. We had to print a different paper to send to the county seat on Friday morning. So I didn't go to school Friday either. I just went to school three days. It's good to have friends in high places. But I was passing all my courses and doin real well.

I graduated in December of that year in a class of two. So, I was either valedictorian or salutatorian. Then, in about February, Ed got drafted into the Air Force Intelligence. He was extremely bright and somehow or another, they figured him for Intelligence.

They only had a lease on the paper. So they got out of their lease, and it was leased to another couple, and I immediately didn't like them and they didn't like me--my smokin, my cursin, whatever. They were super-religious. So I gave em notice and left and went to work at the *Waxahachie Daily News*."

I interrupt Mack's story to call attention to two matters of importance: Mack's attitude toward authority and, a related issue, his attitude toward religiously based rules. The current Republican party would not feel like home to Mack. He next told about hitchhiking to Denton, working various printing jobs, and enrolling at North Texas State College:

"There were only 23 boys at North Texas State when I first went there and about 850 girls, and a nickel bus ride away was TCW, Texas College for Women or something like that. It was a nice place to live.

"In the summer of '44 I was about to turn 18. You couldn't join anything but the army, and the war was winding down. Both of my brothers were drafted into the army, and both warned me, 'Don't join the army. You'll end up in the stockade.'

"I was a smart ass, an upstart. I really was. I'm embarrassed to think of some of the stupid shit I did. But they opened the Merchant Marine up for people who were seventeen and a half. So, another guy and I joined the Merchant Marines and had to report for active duty at the train station there at Dallas at 11:00 a.m. to be sworn in on the platform to catch the damn train. You had to have all your crap in one suitcase.

So we got on the train, just forty-two or forty-three of us and the Petty Officer who sore us in, and a couple of days later I got out in Grand Central Station in New York. And I'd never been nowhere, never read no books, and nobody'd ever told me nothing... [We caught] the shuttle to Times Square, took the subway out to the end of the line out in Brooklyn, and walked a couple of blocks to the Sheep's Head Bay Maritime Base where I took boot training for about six weeks... Then they tested us for different things, and I tested high for math and physics. And they needed radio officers, so they asked me if I wanted to go to radio school, and I said, "Yeah, that's fine."

This young kid who would've been a high school drop out if he'd been allowed, who'd 'never read no books' nor let anybody tell him nothin, still managed to test high in math and physics. If all the details of his story were reported here, the reader would be astounded by what he recalls from seventy years before.

Try to imagine a fourteen year-old Mack taking orders from a Wall Street banker, Mack at seventeen being told what to do by someone like one of the Koch brothers, or Mack at any age letting a preacher tell him what to think.

His story continues after the war years. He talks as if his skills as a printer and machinist were run of the mill, easy to pick up, like those physics and math abilities of his:

"I didn't know I had any math or physics ability till I took that test for the Merchant Marine. So [after the war] I went back to Denton and majored in physics and worked at the *Denton Record Chronicle*. And Moore Business Forms was opening a brand new plant there. I helped spec the typesetting equipment because the foreman didn't know anything about it. We were buying used linotype equipment, so I went with him. Skilled printers were not very available, and I was a machinist too. You had to be to get the damn paper out. Anyhow, I worked there I guess about a year and majored in physics and made really good grades.

At this point Mack gets his introduction to labor unions:

"My friend Ed Bateman (who'd hired him in Currant) was running this big printing business in Dallas, and I'd go over and visit them on the weekends. And I found out they were a union shop, and they were making a lot more money than we were. So I decided to organize a union at Moore Business Cards. I was working at nights there, and I was talking it up. So Ed Bateman had arranged for a rep from the typesetters and the bookbinders union to come on a Sunday afternoon to talk to us and I had gone to the city hall to reserve the auditorium of the public library.

"'Sure fine, Sunday afternoon. What y'all gonna do?" they asked.

"'Union people,' I told them.'"

"Pretty soon it was all over town [that I was trying to unionize] because when I got to work the next afternoon, I went in the employees' entrance. There, next to the punch clock stood the superintendent, the guy I'd traveled with and taught a lot about linotypes. He was standing there and he jumped my ass about my work or something. I reared back and my [cocky attitude came back], and I said, 'Well, if you don't like it, you can get my damn check.'

"He put his arm around me and pulled my check right out of his pocket and ... he walked me about two steps to the employee entrance; and I was out on the street. I had no rights because I had quit; I had gotten my pay, and I was out of a job.

"I thought, 'I'll just go down to the *Chronicle* and get a job.' But there were no jobs in Denton, Texas for a twenty-one year-old war vet and union-organizing printer/machinist... I withdrew from school and took my suitcase back to Dallas and worked for the *Dallas Morning News*. Joined the union."

Then, I decided to go to school down here at UT. I came down to UT in January and moved into Prather Hall. And I went down to the *American Statesman* and joined the union. I'd gotten pretty damn radical at that time. When the contracts had been expired for about three months, I began pushing, "Pull a damn strike. Shut the sonvabitch down!" The union men up in Waco weren't responsive, so called a meeting for Sunday morning. "Boy, I was fired up! I made my speech... so when the vote came, I got 13 votes for a strike, and the vote against got about 65..."

Then he described "pulling his slug" (quitting) and "slugging up" at various jobs in San Antonio, Houston, and finally back in Austin at the American Statesman, which is important because events show (1) Mack is more idealistically driven about unions than most and (2) he's about to meet the woman who would become his wife:

"When I got back, I met a guy named Tannehill. He was an older fella, and he'd been an autoworker during the strikes of the 30's and had gotten bashed on the head in union lines in Detroit, I believe it was. Anyhow, he was a staunch union guy. When I was working in either San Antone (sic) or maybe Houston, two FBI guys came in to investigate me about that vote at the *American Statesman* in Austin. They were asking, "Is this guy a red?"

"And, anyway, Tannehill looked up at them. Here they are in their snap threads and their ties and so forth, and he says it so loud you can hear it all over, 'Git your ass outta here and get a real job!'"

Union men had taken blows and lost lives in their battle against low wages offered by business owners, and apparently the communist-fearing FBI under Hoover had sided against the unions. As the rest of the story will show, even after Mack became a business owner, himself, he never relinquished his view that the men who devoted their time and sweat to putting out the product--the car, the paper, whatever the product--were indispensable and as valuable as the financing which a banker or a wealthy owner might provide.

The second lesson from this statement made by the head-injured Tannehill is loyalty, especially loyalty among the people of the working class when the rich and powerful try to fight unionization.

I do not know if the history of labor is currently taught in Texas high schools. Perhaps it is taught just as the Civil War is taught, by the same teachers who apparently teach that "the Civil War wasn't about slavery." A man of Mack's age must remind us that non-unionized New York seamstresses were making wages equivalent to current Pakistanis, that in the 1870's railroad construction workers had to pay all of their expenses out of $30 per month, or that Robber Baron Jay Gould bragged that he could break a strike by hiring "half the working class to kill the other half." With so many Republicans decidedly anti-union, it is unlikely Mack could find a Republican candidate to support. Meanwhile, Mack was headed back to school at the University of Texas. He explains:

"I went back to school and switched over to Economics. That semester I took nothing but five Econ courses, and Ann (his future wife) was in Comparative Economics with me. Sure enough, I fell for her the minute I saw her. A buddy had been dating her and said he couldn't get anywhere, so he set me up with her. 'You're both squares. Maybe you'll get along,' he told me.

"And we did get along, but come November I get a call that my sister was dying in Dallas. She'd been fifteen when I was born. She used to carry me around on her hip. I was her doll.

I include this in his story to remind us how Mack values loyalty:

"She had come out of Mayo Clinic and was at the Hoxsey Cancer clinic in Dallas. She was there maybe a month, but they finally told her, 'There's no hope' and sent her home. When I heard that, I just got up and paid my bills and didn't even withdraw from the university. I was so upset that I went to Dallas, moved into a cheap hotel, went to work at the *Dallas News*, and spent every spare minute with my sister at the clinic. When she moved back home to Corsicana, I'd work about three days a week at the *Times Herald*, enough to pay my bills, and spend the rest of the time in Corsicana. My mother and father were both alive at that time, and I lived with them but visited my sister's house as much as I could. I was sitting up with her the night she died. She was thirty-seven.

A little before my sister died, my father turned out to have cancer of the breast. He had fallen along a barbed wire fence as a kid, 'wraslin with some kid. Cut him pretty good. Had a big scar. It turned cancerous and he went into the hospital and came home and died at home.

Sis had died in January of '51; dad, in July. When I left U.T. that day to go to see my sister in Dallas, I never went back to school. I was trying like hell to get married and make some money.

To make money, Mack continued working in the printing business, but now he became an owner. Mack doesn't belabor the point, but events reveal the vulnerability of working people, people unable to amass wealth or afford insurance:

At this time, my friend, Ed, whom I'd worked for at thirteen, had come to own the Marr printing company, but he developed an unusual type of epilepsy. When he went into a clinic, the employees asked me to come and run that shop. They were good printers, but not business types. I leased it. I'd go to work at 3:00 in the morning. Did all of my back shop work till noon. I was exhausted but I could take a five or ten minute nap and rise like new bread.

I did that everyday. And then I'd go down, run the office and do my pricing and billing or binding work where you didn't get ink on you. I had a good secretary, and I'd visit customers and that sort of thing.

My dad died on the 26th of July, and in October my friend, Ed, had gotten out of the hospital. He was recuperating and didn't know exactly when he'd be ready to go back to work, but he felt good. He loved to garden and he was gonna go outside gardening one day, and I was gonna come by and take him to lunch. I get home and take my shower and about the time I'm gettin out of the shower I get a phone call that my friend died, and so I went straight to the hospital; but, sure enough, he was gone.

I moved to Austin and got married four days later. Didn't have a job. Had some money. Had a nice car. I wasn't worried about a job. I mean, I could work anywhere. There were so many union shops where I could work at that time."

Union shops gave a man mobility and a measure of security, not that Mack was ever afraid to roll the dice and make a move. Life was just beginning for Mack and Ann and, eventually, their five children. He had many adventures to recount, but much of my questions have been answered regarding what convinces a man to not to vote for a party favored by bankers and anyone else who is willing to profit from the desperation of workers. At this point in his life, he started his own machinist business while working as a printer for the American Statesman. Needless to say, he was again working around the clock. Here is a typical description:

"To make extra money, I was maintaining linotypes. I had ten under contracts here in Austin, five for one typesetting company and two in a little Swedish newspaper, and five at AC Baldwin, of course. I'd go these three places and read the notes they'd left, and I'd clean em and then get home about the time my kids were having breakfast. Then I'd sleep till about three in the afternoon. We'd go out to Barton Creek and swim and picnic, and then at 10:00 I'd go to work at the *American Statesman.*"

After much juggling of ventures and adventures, Mack was eventually able to start his own printing shop. Despite his being the owner, it was a union shop, the only 100% union shop. He and his partner, Jim:

"We really worked our asses off, and we had by then six or seven employees, and we had to make that payroll every week and we'd be sweating bullets to make the payroll on Friday, and then Jim and I would sit down to see if we had enough money to make it through the weekend. I'd say, 'I got to have $35 to buy groceries.' He'd look through the invoices and he'd say, 'You take these two. They're on your way home, and I think you can get those. And I'll take these.' We'd collect a little money on the way home. That's how we were living at that time. My wife could somehow put up with it. Ann was a wonderful, wonderful human being."

His printing business evolved into a computer business in 1967 after zip codes started and instead of using the alphabet to order mail, it required mail to be organized by zip codes.

In 1972, we bought our first Hewlett Packard. Customers rented time on computer. We had doubled memory size within one year and leased computer time on twenty-eight terminals with high speed modems around town, all with automated billing. *Struggling to master various programs needed for their computer business, Mack explains:*

"I took the printout of the RPG program and worked backwards till I understood. Then, one morning, December 26 it was, we were real busy, lots competition, and I taking a shower and suddenly wondered why there was no universal program. So wrote it in numbers, 500 lines of code, and it would do simple jobs. It was a great program for running a data center.

I was still writing the program in '79. It eventually used five parameters and grew to 28100 lines of code. In the late '70s, I presented the program at a conference in Switzerland. But that's when the PC came along, and data centers weren't necessary after that.

I sold the company to my employees in '86. When they held their first board meeting, they voted down the union. "We're owners. Who would we bargain with?"

Finally, Mack has retired. I ask him to reflect, "You're the guy who sees all of these business opportunities, and you benefitted from you entrepreneurship, but you consider yourself a socialist," and he takes us back to that first printing company in his hometown of Corsicana where he worked at thirteen:

I became a Socialist at fourteen at the printing shop in Corsicana. I was changing the partial magazine at the bottom of the linotype and was about to put it on the linotype, and it suddenly hit me that, 'This thing is a f***ing racket.' I took the magazine and sort of laid it on the top of my head for a minute to get my thoughts together and I pulled all the goddamned brass mats out of that magazine, 200 of em, and dumped em on the f***ing floor, so yeah, I remember it quite well. And I had to pick all them up and feed them back into the automatic distribution system.

Question: What was a racket?

"The whole economy. See, my dad was working for the city water department, and that helped me put it together. That was a public utility, and the banks were a racket. I had a distant uncle who was an officer in one of the banks there in Corsicana. He was my grandmother's brother. We never knew them. They lived on the other side of town, if you know what I mean.

We couldn't afford a phone at that time. Before we could afford a Frigidaire with a "Money miser" daily payment of $.25/day to pay for it, I was the kid who had to run down to the icehouse and get 15 pound block of ice every day.

This hard-working child of hard-working parents--smart, loyal, lacking nothing but the wealth of the relative who lived on the rich side of town--he didn't think inescapable poverty had to be the natural order of things.

He said, "I remember thinking the telephone company ought to be a damned public utility.

Is Mack a Yeller Dawg because he wants the government to take care of him, this man who struck out on his own as a cocky fourteen year-old, who never ran short of the intelligence to learn anything he needed to do--from printing, to computer programming--who never ran out of courage to try anything, who never ran out of energy to work around the clock, not till at eighty-nine he finds himself bedridden by a quadruple bypass? No, he just never wanted to go through life as anybody's fool, didn't want to work for peanuts so other men could get rich for approving loans.

Getting handouts isn't the issue that drives Mack's politics. He sees capitalism as a racket to take advantage of the little guy like him, like his father. It made him pro-union and anti-bank, not a great leap for a man who'd always been independent. Gun rights, abortion rights, civil rights--these weren't the issues that shaped his thinking, though he certainly wouldn't support subjugation of anyone. And it certainly wasn't shaped by a sermon he heard in church. A child of the depression and a World War II vet, he taught himself printing, machining, and writing computer code. Something of a prodigy, he progressed from gofer to printer to business owner to champion of the working man who would have been at the mercy of business owners and bankers if it weren't for unions and business owners like him.

Calling Mack a "prodigy" reminds me of an old joke, or at least its punch line. There's a highly educated Yankee who thinks he's a lot smarter that the drawling Texas oilman, and in the punchline the Texan asks, "Well if you're so smart, why aren't you as rich as me?" Clearly, Mack had a strong drive to learn, to earn a living, then to support his family; but never in his story did he mention getting rich. He did talk a lot about economic justice, though.

Chapter 4: A Woman's Place[6]

Jane explained, "My mother was a homemaker who had to work to support the family due to my father's illness." This daughter of a persevering homemaker can speak for herself and makes clear how faith, knowledge, and reason can coexist and create values and opinions which prevent someone from finding shelter under the Republican tent.

Interviewer: "You're a Texan, Jane, but you don't vote Republican. Why not? How do your life experiences differ from the typical Texas Republican?"

Jane: "I discussed politics with my father as a teen. He was Republican, a racist, and a sexist. Republicans don't want to study, learn, adapt, and be future-oriented. He spoke of egalitarian values, but he acted quite to the contrary, much like Republicans who love to wrap themselves in Christian values but support the death penalty and oppose help for people struggling with unemployment or drugs or just bad luck."

Interviewer: "You said Republicans don't want to learn, think, and adapt. Can you explain how you learned to value education, reason, and so forth?"

"I went to college over my father's objections because he thought a college education was wasted on women. I liked the experience. My horizons were expanded. For the first time, I was going to school with blacks as well as students from other countries and ethnicities. I became a political activist in college and have continued to this day--my desire for education and the opportunity to form opinions on issues and lobby, speak, write, and demonstrate for them. I became acquainted with feminism and the civil rights movement.

"I knew I didn't want to settle for being just a secretary or a clerk, but I didn't yet have an occupation formed in my mind. I changed my major four times – from mathematics to teaching to marketing (business), finally settling on sociology. Then I went on to get a Masters in Public Health. Among my cousins, I was the only one, male or female, to graduate from college and get an advanced degree."

Interviewer: "When we were talking, you asked, 'How can women vote for Republicans and against their own interests?' What did you mean?"

Jane: "Republican do not support equal pay, a living wage, any increases in the minimum wage, parental leave, free child-care, food stamps, job training or education subsidies, increases in Social Security or Medicaid, workplace

---

[6] Author's Note: This interview began in person but was finished in writing. Some phrasing was changed for the sake of clarity.

protection, unionization, or for women to have control of their reproductive choice. All of these policies would more greatly benefit women because women are trapped in lower-paying jobs, leave the workforce to care for children and relatives, because unions help women get equal pay and better jobs, because women more often depend solely on social security in retirement because they haven't been able to save because they are cheated out of fair wages.

"Trump is popular because he talks about simplistic solutions. His solutions don't work very well in a democratic society. Trump talks tough about solving terrorism by sending hundreds of thousands of our soldiers over to the Mideast. His solution has been tried and failed. Terrorists are already here. They are us--frightened, resentful, alienated, and raging to make others feel their pain.

"Trump is used to having people kowtow to his whims because of his celebrity and what he gets away with in the business environment. But governing a country involves many constituencies with varying power and involvement in policy. For example, a President has to negotiate with the Congressional opponents even when it is controlled by his own party.

"Much of our problems with other nations are the result of our meddling. We've invaded sovereign nations in the guise of bringing democracy to them. Some religious beliefs held by some Republicans are antithesis to democracy because they do not want to recognize women or other ethnicities as equals. Our future as a nation is in more jeopardy from falling behind technologically than from foreign jihadists."

Interviewer: "What other values do you hold which are contrary to the Republicans?"

Jane: "Republicans talk about being pro life but they do not value the life of children once they are born. They oppose food stamps, free childcare, child friendly business environments, free college and improving public education. Republicans want tax laws to favor business at the cost of public services. A mantra of Republicanism is to privatize everything. In the end, it usually costs more, there's little accountability, and it does not benefit the common good. A proliferation of guns has not made America safer from crime or terrorism...

"We aren't [taking into consideration] those people who don't want guns in public places, who... [feel threatened by] gun enthusiasts. I compare that to the anti-smoking campaign. Until a certain behavior is recognized for the harm it does to most people just to indulge a few, we will have too many guns."

Interviewer: "I don't think there are any religious fundamentalists in this group. What are your religious beliefs?"

Jane: "I think what we perceive as the human experience is but the subjective result of our thought. Although we appear to be born, live, and then die, our mortal experience is but a phase of our thought. I recognize more dimensions than just four. "

Interviewer's note: Jane was explaining her view that we have a spiritual level of existence that transcends the physical life we experience in our four dimensional life in time and in three-dimensional space. She considers our time-limited, physical life to be all that our minds can directly experience.

She went on to say, "In the spiritual sphere of being, our life is eternal with God who is unchanging good. That doesn't mean we can ignore the material world... [during the time] we appear to be a part of it. We... [can see there is more] if we pay attention. Otherwise, how can you account for extra-sensory-perception, intuition, or *deja vu*?

"I believe that God is always speaking to us, enlightening, guiding and caring for us. We just choose not to listen or to acknowledge. [The Republican party is]... populated by evangelical voters, those who believe in the literal interpretation of the Bible and draw their values from a... [myth of creation] involving Adam and a seductive Eve.

"Take for instance the problem of climate change. Republican spokesmen deny the threat of... warming to the Earth and oceans, discounting research by the majority of experts. This directly serves the oil and gas companies that want to continue to make billions out of exploiting the earth. Climate change deniers, whose experts are few and backed by oil companies, have lulled them into thinking the climate change is a hoax, that... [the temperature change is] no more than a slight aberration, and [no matter what] we are experiencing (storms, floods, earthquakes), somehow God will intervene; and, miraculously, we will all be saved. Republicans think that somehow without [our] doing anything, the Earth will right itself. They cannot reconcile their belief in an all-seeing, all-powerful God with His letting humankind destroy itself. Even in business vernacular (such as insurance forms), we attribute storms, earthquakes and hurricanes to God's will.

"Some humans cling to an anthropomorphic God who exacts vengeance and bestows good things based on unfathomable motives. We should not be so ignorant. There is always an explanation for a [physical] event. The more we understand about our material existence, the less superstitious and irrational we are.

"Technology is frightening to those who resist change and cling to outgrown values and attitudes. However, technology is a result of inspired thought, hard work, and commitment to a purpose. The appliances, conveyances, and progress in communication are fantastic when viewed by persons of, say, a hundred years ago. Imagine what ease will be available in another hundred. It's almost a fairytale existence.

"I believe that God is always speaking to us, enlightening, guiding, and caring for us. We just choose not to listen, or acknowledge. I reference a joke about a person who drowned and came before God and asked why He hadn't saved him. God reminded him that He'd sent someone with a canoe to his door, but the man had said, 'No, God will save me.' When the waters rose, God sent someone in a boat to his second story window, but he said, 'No, God will save me.' Finally he sent a helicopter to his rooftop, but the stubborn man said he would wait for God to save him, so he drowned. God said, 'You ignored all my efforts to save you.'

"I see the Republican leaders appealing to people's fears about the future and change. Human emotions [like fear and hate] retard our growth and cause friction that results in wars and disruption. There is no perfect time [to which we can] return. We need to be tolerant of differences and not so quick to judge by appearances."

I don't think Jane will be getting any invitations to a Republican's Women's Group soon.

Chapter 5: The Cheater

When Brian's parents brought their first son home from the hospital, they were living in a converted chicken coop. Before moving in, his dad had swept the pen-feathers off the plank walls, scooped out the chicken poop, and rolled out a strip of linoleum on top of the dirt. Central Texas is hot in the summer, even for those who live in a two-story house where the heat can rise, but chicken coops don't have two stories; and in 1940, window air conditioners were unknown among chicken coops. Brian's parents couldn't even afford a fan.

In seventh grade, Brian showed up at Austin's old Allen Junior High. Since Blacks attended segregated schools until high school, he attended school with Mexicans and other poor, working-class White kids.

Like them, Brian's mind focused on things other than school. But unlike most of his friends, he read. At that time he was reading the Tarzan series. At bedtime, he would make up his own stories and tell them to his two younger brothers. One series anticipated Ant Man and told of the adventures of a very small superhero who lived in the "Land of the Mouse People."

But once he got to school, Brian was in warrior mentality. Those were mean streets, those dirt roads of east Austin. Few of his cohort are alive today; and he explained that "Anybody who is alive, probably wears a numbered shirt."[7]

Today Brian is a seasoned novelist, but back then he paid very little attention to his bored, discouraged English teacher's droning on at the front of the class. One day his teacher assigned the class a story to write. For once, Brian had an assignment that interested him, and he had no trouble writing up an adventure-packed story, well-organized from its inciting event through its tense crisis to its uplifting conclusion in which the hero defeats the forces of evil. He turned it in, and went on about his business.

Later that day, the English teacher pulled him out of the class and told him, "You didn't write this. You plagiarized this story, young man."

"What's *plagiarized* mean?"

"You stole it from another writer."

---

[7] Meaning he is incarcerated.

"No, I didn't."

"Yes, you did. Take this sentence." She read from the hand-written two-page story. "That phrasing. No one from your class could write like that."

"But I did write it."

"Well, I know you didn't. So, you have two choices: You can take an F, or you can admit you plagiarized it, and I'll give you a C."

Brian shrugged, figured it was useless to argue. He was really more concerned about the gang of Mexican boys who were planning to beat up his younger brother after school. "Okay, I didn't write it," he lied and took the C.

Two weeks after turning seventeen, Brian left school to join the Navy. He'd finished his tour and was a civilian again when Vietnam started heating up. Feeling the call to duty, he re-enlisted, this time in the army. After passing a battery of mental and physical tests, including the eight-week jump school at Fort Benning, he reached the Special Forces Training Group at Fort Bragg. Possessing a fighter pilot's (or a good major league baseball hitter's) better-than-20-20 eyesight, Brian proved to be one of the best shots among the new recruits; plus, he had excelled in the tests of survival skills.

Still, when he came before a promotion board at one point during the second year into his second enlistment, he was not its first choice. The board didn't want to promote unmarried Brian. They had someone else in mind, a man supporting a wife and two children. But passing Brian over for promotion proved complicated: The team of sergeants giving the oral exam had to find a plausible excuse for disqualifying him. Weapon ranges, muzzle velocities, range and capability of artillery—he knew it all.

They grilled him for two hours before they could find a question he couldn't answer. They kept asking questions until finally the board asked him the number on the form used to request a three-day pass. Finding something he didn't know, they gave the promotion to the other soldier. When Brian found out the reason, he agreed with the Board: The other soldier was supporting a family and needed the raise more than he did.

In the early 60's his Texas drawl and uncompromising attitude earned him challenges from some of his African-American, fellow soldiers. He didn't look for the fights and bore no racial prejudice, but the stocky pitbull had grown up in the mean streets of east Austin where his adversaries were most often gangs of Hispanics, rather than Blacks. Brian had learned never to back down, so in the army he left bigger men beaten and damaged in his wake. This may have contributed to Brian's not playing the part of promotion material.

In other situations, he could play a part quite well. After the Army, Brian tried his hand at acting and eventually won a scholarship to London's Royal

Academy of Dramatic Arts, but he turned it down. He didn't want to postpone marrying the woman he loved.

Instead of studying acting in London, Brian worked in high-rise construction, fathered two sons, and invested in land north of Austin, Texas, recently America's fastest growing city. Having entered the world dirt poor, literally dirt poor, he had served his country in both the Navy and the Army and excelled as a soldier and an actor. After discharge, he rose from union carpenter to union foreman to union general foreman to union superintendent; and when, in his words, "the Republicans collapsed the construction unions," he moved his book over to the millwright union where he finished out his career.

Brian doesn't identify with those who were "to the manor born." He identifies instead with the workingman. So, Brian is clearly not a "pointy headed intellectual," as Spiro Agnew used to say. He is not a peacenik from the sixties, in fact quite the opposite--with no threat from the draft, he re-enlisted and went into training with the Army's Special Forces.

One might ask, "If he identifies with the working man, could he be a real Texan?"

Answer: Beginning on January 1, 2016 when Texas' new law comes into effect, Brian intends to wear his sidearm in a visible holster in. You can't get more Texan than that. So, does Brian vote Republican? He can answer for himself, especially if provoked, and that's my job.

Searching for the fuse to set off an explosion of Brian's convictions, I told him that one of my interviewees had been a Republican, and all her friends were Republican. I asked her, "The South was solidly Democratic till the '60's. What didn't your friends and neighbors in Virginia like about the Democrats?"

She told me, "I think it was because of the hand-outs."

Now, you have to understand that Brian's response to this answer comes from a workingman who came up scraping to survive:

"Not all Democrats are about hand-outs if that's what you call food stamps and ADC—though I understand how it got started and why. That was LBJ. And the kids of Blacks and poor Whites were starving, f*****g starving. The workingmen in this country just want jobs and a living wage. A f*****g living wage, not a f*****g WalMart minimum wage, or working an eighteen-hour day just to put food on the table so Sam Walton's heirs can line museum walls with multimillion dollar paintings.

"I know people who are holding three jobs and can't make enough to buy food. They are starving to death while heads of corporations and bankers have billions. It's not right.

"Donald Trump will say, 'My father just gave me a little help, and I did the rest, myself.' 'A little help,' Trump says. A million bucks! And then he whined because his daddy made him pay it back. There were tears in his eyes when he added, 'with interest.' F**k him! When I left home, my dad gave me five bucks, which he had to force on me. I didn't want to take it. To a workingman, what Trump got is more than *a little* help. He got the kind of head start you get in a marathon when they put your starting point ten feet from the finish line. And even then he had to cheat—four times."

In other words, don't talk about dealing with poverty if you really don't know anything about it. Brian does. His mom came home from the hospital with him to a chicken coop in central Texas with not even a fan to move the hot air when summer came.

Brian was on a roll: "I think there should be higher taxes for people who make money off of other people's money, you know the guys who figure out how to rob pension funds, get their running-dog cronies in Washington to bail them out with taxpayer money, which adds to the national debt. Then they give themselves multi-million dollar bonuses for pulling off the biggest bank job in history. And those tax dollars should go to healthcare and infrastructure and military and unemployment insurance, as well as social security--which we, the people who actually do the work, finance from our first paycheck to our last. Republicans want to take social security away, and do what instead?

"Bush II wanted to put people's retirement in the hands of stockbrokers and insurance agents. Where the f**k would everybody over sixty-five be now, all those old f**ks who voted Republican. If you don't own a plane or can't afford to own one, and you still vote Republican, you deserve what you get."

This was one of Brian's calmer, more reasoned responses. It showed his identification with the working man who puts in a day's work for a day's pay. He isn't greedy, has a conscience, cares about justice, fairness, patriotism, and extending a help to those fellow Americans who need and deserve it. He grew up a poor White, and identifies with the working man even though he now qualifies as an upper-middle-class landowner and landlord. He judges men by their work ethic and character, not skin color, or religion, nationality, or bank account.

"What do you think about the Republican candidates?" I needled.

"The Republicans are about to nominate that dingleberry who thinks the world started six thousand years ago..." he began. (This reference was to Ben Carson before his drop in the polls.)

There was another matter of justice that he hadn't mentioned. Despite his seventh grade teacher's doubts, Brian was and still is a storyteller. He has recently authored a story that bubbled up from his psychic outrage with the

Whiteman's treatment of Native Americans. He suffers no illusions that the Apache and Comanche would have peaceably turned over their buffalo-hunting grounds to invading White farmers. And, warrior that he is, he admits he would have shot and killed marauding Apaches.

Knowing this, I asked about the views of our country's continued treatment of Native Americans, which fueled his latest (as-yet unpublished) novel, *Geronimo's Bones*: "In your book, you didn't romanticize the Indian. You don't portray him as nice to White folk or gladly coexisting with all those White people planting crops where the buffalo once roamed. But you don't go along with the genocide either. Republicans talk about bleeding-heart liberals, but you might be the least bleeding-heart person I know. Yet our treatment of the Indian offends you."

I then sat back with my recorder and got an ear-full for my efforts:

"My thing is 'what's done is done,' but stop f*****g over the Indians. Stop going on to their lands to take their coal and their oil. Stop making deals to dig up their goddam land if its got copper on it and just giving them a pittance of the f*****g money. Just f*****g stop! That's what I'm saying."

"And do what instead?"

"Make their land sovereign. If we really want to make things right, we need to go back up into Oklahoma and buy up all the goddam land that we divided into a checkerboard when we took it from the Kiowas and the Comanches and the Apaches. They ended up losing their quarter sections because they couldn't pay the land taxes that the f*****g federal and state government put on then. We should give that land back to them. We took all the rest. People say, "Oh, we can't do that," but "yes, you f*****g can. You can go give ten billion f*****g dollars a year to Israel. You can spend three f*****g trillion dollars beating a bunch of f*****g ragheads to death and then not even do a very good job of it. I mean where in the f***k is genocide when you need it?!"

"Where is genocide when you need it?" he'd asked (and I assume he meant genocide of the White land-grabbers). I feel quite proud of myself for provoking this tirade, having heard parts of it before but needing to hear it again for transcription purposes, not to mention its high entertainment value. Since Brian has just suggested genocide, we can conclude that the accused literary cheat has no stomach for a Republican sense of justice.

How will Brian be dismissed?

Does he seek handouts? He never received any.

Is he unpatriotic? Don't tell him to his face, not this veteran of both the Army and the Navy.

Does he envy the rich? Why would he? He rose from poverty to amass substantial land holdings?

No, he values work, patriotism, honor, loyalty, and not one Republican candidate.

Chapter 6: Son of a Preacher Man

My talented warrior-writer-friend, Brian, might never have taken a chemistry class at Harvard like Al Gore, but he can think logically; and before we move on to the next Yeller Dawg, this is what he had to say about climate change: "The oil companies try to cast doubt, but how can we not be responsible for climate change. For a couple of hundred years, we've been burning more fossil fuels and sending more carbon dioxide into the atmosphere. Carbon dioxide is a greenhouse gas, meaning that just like the glass in a greenhouse, it prevents the release of heat from the air into outer space. We might not know how bad it's going to get, but we follow the logic that burning fossil fuels makes it worse."[8]

In response to my request for information, Yeller Dawg Roy sent me some information about his work as an environmentalist. I'd already stumbled onto his most recent endeavor to save the planet, a presentation about a university geology professor's effort to warn the Texas legislature that our state's drought preparation plan was inadequate.

The professor showed us data--geological data, historical data, meteorological data. We sat in the pews nodding in agreement with the logic of his argument. Not surprisingly, the legislative committee--dominated by

---

[8] For those who know that something paradoxical is taking place over Antarctica, I quote *Science News*, 12/4/15, "CO_2 absorbs and emits heat in the form of infrared radiation. When infrared radiation emanating from Earth's relatively warm surface hits a CO_2 molecule in the atmosphere, the molecule can absorb the energy and later reemit it as infrared radiation. Like a pinball machine, the CO_2 molecule fires the infrared energy in a random direction. Sometimes, the emitted energy continues out into space, but other times it returns to the surface, creating warming called the greenhouse effect.

Satellites monitor the amount of radiation escaping into space. Where CO_2 blocks radiation from the surface, scientists see a dip in the amount of escaping infrared radiation. Over the Antarctic Plateau in the center of the icy continent, satellites instead see an increase in the infrared radiation escaping into space within the range of frequencies associated with CO_2.

This negative greenhouse effect, Notholt and colleagues propose, results from the region's frigid temperatures, the coldest on Earth (*SN: 1/25/14, p. 15*). The Antarctic Plateau sits at a high elevation at the southernmost part of the globe and is covered by sunlight-reflecting ice and snow. Temperatures on the ground can drop as low as −93.2° Celsius and are typically colder than those in the stratosphere 20 kilometers or more up.

The ground is so cold that little infrared radiation comes from the planet's surface. But, like in other places around the world, CO_2 in the stratosphere over Antarctica soaks in heat in the atmosphere and sends infrared radiation pinballing in different directions. That siphons some heat into space that would otherwise stay near Earth. Elsewhere, this effect is normally overshadowed by the trapping of heat from the ground, but in Antarctica, so little heat comes from the ground that the loss becomes significant, causing an overall cooling effect."

Republicans, since they were all elected in the state of Texas--rejected his suggestion for more aggressive drought preparations.

But we were surprised to learn that the argument which defeated science consisted of one sentence: "According to the Bible, God created the earth for man's benefit; He did not create man to take care of the earth."

This argument may not have surprised Roy as much as me. He explained that his father was a fundamentalist minister who changed congregations several times as Roy was growing up, so Roy started life in the Midwest but graduated from a Texas high school and won a scholarship to attend college in Texas. In his words, "I left home and went to college and began to read books and talked to people. I learned how the current Bible was constructed, all the books that were left out, and all the translations. Plus, my roommate was a good person even though he wasn't religious.

"When I came home for Christmas break, my father didn't want me to go back. He explained that the downfall of man began when he ate of the fruit of the tree of knowledge. Knowledge is therefore the root of all evil. So, I guess I will go to Hell, which I don't believe in. When I did continue my education, he basically disowned me. "

After retirement Roy and his wife moved to a new Texas city and put into practice the things they had been reading about the conservation of energy. Their house is powered by solar panels, and water is preserved. The yard of their home has been certified as a backyard wildlife habitat. He drives a solar powered car.

Due to their energy saving efforts, their solar panels produce electricity to heat and cool their home, heat their water, and charge their electric car, so they now live completely off the power grid. It's been four years since Roy and his wife have paid a bill to the power company. He's never had to pay for maintenance on his car, and he hasn't bought a drop of gas in four years. "So far, I still produce more electricity than I use each month so I am driving on sunshine which is free," said Roy.

At this point I became curious about the official Republican position on the environment. Per www.gop.com/platform/americas-natural-resources/, the GOP favors the following:

"The Republican Party is committed to domestic energy independence... Advancing technology has given us a more accurate understanding of the nation's enormous reserves that are ours for the development. The role of public officials must be to encourage responsible development across the board. Unlike the current Administration, we will not pick winners and losers in the energy marketplace. Instead, we will let the free market and the public's preferences determine the industry outcomes. In assessing the various sources of potential energy, Republicans advocate an all-of-the-above diversified approach, taking advantage of all our American God-given resources. That is the best way to advance North American energy independence."

In the Republican view, carbon fuels are a resource, a product to be bought and sold, its consumption based a market forces. The platform contains no mention of "climate change," a.k.a, "global warming." It appears that followers of the Republican platform will resist any efforts to cap oil wells, board up coal mines, or turn instead to the "renewable sources of energy." They say, "We encourage the cost-effective development of renewable energy, but the taxpayers should not serve as venture capitalists for risky endeavors. It is important to create a pathway toward a market-based approach for renewable energy sources..."

The platform goes on to voice support for a "strong and stable energy sector" relying on gas, oil, coal, and even "alternative sources for electricity generation such as wind, hydro, solar, biomass, geothermal, and tidal energy"--not a bad thing, sustainability, sounds reasonable, but perhaps not ambitious enough for someone who sees the world headed for uninhabitability.

Lacking any mention of CO2 levels or climate change, this platform doesn't sound appealing to Roy and his wife. They have long-since embraced the information which has been discovered since the Bible was written.

Chapter 7: Facing the Folks Back Home

When I met Caleb, he was writing fiction. In one novel a young man leaves west Texas to become a writer in New York. It was just a story, of course, but John did grow up in west Texas, and he did like to write, and he was making an impression on the New York literary scene until a mysterious fire destroyed a building full of his writings. Perhaps the mystery of this event affected the tone of his writing. Perhaps all of his experiences after leaving west Texas pushed him away from the beliefs held by most of his fellow west Texans:

"I grew up in this little pocket in the backwaters of society. In the west Texan's view America, God and west Texas come first. If you are on the left, you are some kind of an idiot. All my Republicans friends think Democrats are one step away from Communism, and the Democrats think Republicans are one step away from Fascism. I saw this survey: As a group, Republicans hate change and like the status quo. In my experience, this means, Me and mine come first.' I don't know why that is.

"I talked with my cousin while I was visiting out there. My cousin doesn't believe in climate change. I tried to disagree with her, but I didn't get through. She just couldn't take in the information."

I interrupt Caleb to remind the reader of our previous non-Republican, Roy, whose fundamentalist-minister father didn't want him to read any book but the Bible. The message: Forget science; forget technological advances; forget reason, itself, for that matter. All one needs is faith, a blind faith in the words written in the Bible as they were translated into English by completely impartial, divinely inspired translator-scholars.

I do not mock this position. It may turn out to be true. Human reason may not direct us to the ultimate truth. I understand that. (See, *Entangled--a journey through the unknowable* by this author.) But I do have a problem with the Republican politicians who try to have it both ways. A Yale-educated neurosurgeon accepts the scientific method in his work but kicks it aside when facing voters who cannot accept the science behind evolution. Caleb rejects such candidates as hypocrites and won't vote for them, but his cousin doesn't worry about global warming. She has salvation on her mind.

None of Caleb's relatives wanted to know about either his art or his writing: "When I went back to visit, my cousin only wanted to know if I'd been saved. That's all that mattered, not my writing. I told her I had questions that haven't been answered. Of course, she has no questions. She accepts everything on faith, so she is superior to anyone who doesn't." Caleb says, "Out there, we were hypnotized from birth. We went to the Baptist church three times a week--Wednesday night, Sunday morning, and Sunday night prayer meeting."

He offered an interesting hypothesis about the power of fundamentalist preaching: "I think people believe what they are taught if they can be made to feel an emotional surge as they learn. These ideas then become the things that we tell ourselves during times of intense emotion. I see it happening with ISIS, with revolutions like those by Castro or Hitler. Such leaders move people with hellfire and brimstone. They scare them, speak to their fears, and then hypnotize them with the answer, the ideology, they want to impart. I grew up in that milieu, with everybody you know in the same mindset, repeating the same pat answers chapter and verse. That's what Republicans do.

"It affected me too, and it took a long time to shed their influence. For a long time, I worried I was following the ways of the devil. I was out of that environment, but I still believed what they'd taught me, and I suffered from angst. And I still suffer from this moral dilemma about the violent, dark stuff in my writing. I know what they would think, what they would tell me: 'You should be reading the Bible, not writing.'"

Caleb raises a largely unuttered question: How can the avowed fundamentalist politicians claim to employ logic and reason? When will they just blindly, unquestioningly follow Bible teachings, and when will they think about the secular concerns like, for example, the long-term survival of the species? The Donald is a pragmatist, but when do Marco Rubio and Ted Cruz think the Bible should be put aside and human reason should be used to solve problems? They can say that the science behind the hypothesis of human-generated climate change is unconvincing, but can they tell us under what circumstances they'd accept the science? What about the science that warns us of fallout from a nuclear reactor? Should we not worry about inspecting reactors?

And can they explain how, if the scientists did convince them that climate represented a danger to the country (if not the entire world), they would take action to protect the planet? This would be a difficult situation for the Republican candidate because if he some time in the future acknowledged the need for reducing CO_2 emissions, he'd sound like a Democrat arriving late to the party; and if he said he would reject the science regardless of the evidence, he'd lose the respect of all but the most convinced fundamentalist and the most greedy short-term profit seeker.

I suspect these candidates do not suffer from Caleb's angst. They seem not to care if the planet fries in a hundred years. Caleb does care. He doesn't want to win an election. He wants to capture humanity in a phrase. He wants to show us the truth, and he isn't satisfied with the Bible's version of history and science. Once he'd left west Texas, there was no going back to reciting old versus which no longer rang true.

Chapter 8: A Lost Sense of Community

Caleb left his community behind when he traveled from west Texas to New York City. On the other hand, Carrie grew up going to school with every type of kid in the community and then also left her home. Now, having educated herself, worked, traveled, and moved to suburbia, she finds herself segregated in an urban crowd. Here is how she explains it:

"This is a topic I have been thinking about a lot lately. I have been thinking about how we live in silos; and unless we make a strong effort, we never meet an 'other.'

"In previous centuries, the rich and poor came into contact with one another. Small-town schools educated the physician's son along with the sons and daughters of judges, factory workers, and day laborers. Through the draft, men met people from other regions of the country with different worldviews.

"This is no longer true and hasn't been since the Vietnam war when middle and upper class kids could get deferments. And today with the growth of suburbia we live in segregated neighborhoods--economically, racially, educationally segregated.

"Also, there seems to be a belief in conspiracies so that, while more info is available, less of it is believed. And the corollary is true: Really far-out lies, easily debunked, are perceived as truth, especially if they are spoken by the 'truth tellers,' Rush, Glenn and Sean.

"Carrie," I asked, "Where and when did you grow up in this integrated community?"

"I grew up in New Jersey and graduated from high school in 1959. The community was integrated on a financial and class level, not racially or ethnically. In our racially homogenous town, the few (exotic) post WWII immigrant adults were likely Italian or Polish. There were few Protestants and few Jews. I never heard any anti-Semitic statements until I went to work in NYC after college.

"I come from a very Democratic family, but my father had no trouble voting for Ike. Having lived abroad for twenty-two years, I was out of the fray. But the post-2000 elections woke me to the dangers of apathy and ignorance. I am appalled at what we have become."

Growing up in a racially, religiously, and ethnically homogenous community, Carrie had no experience with our great divides.[9] She looks for an explanation in our housing patterns. They segregate us, much like the Great Plains segregates Caleb's native west Texas from outsiders. She challenges us to encounter an "other," and one wonders how many Republican partisans crave contact with someone with different skin color, different beliefs, different sexuality, different language. Caleb didn't think you'd find them in west Texas. And can Republican politicians care about such different people?

---

[9] For a fictional treatment, see "The Great Divide," by the author.

Chapter 9: A Descendant of Slaves

Trick Question: Why would a black man born in New York's Bronx borough after World War II grow up mistrusting the American political economic system?

Trick Answer: How could he grow up otherwise?

(If the reader doesn't understand that answer, he has not known any baby boomers of African American descent. He/she should find some and ask them about their experiences with White society. If he is not curious about how American democracy is working out for a fellow American, he is likely not a Yeller Dawg.)

After our interview, Mack had begun inviting selected Yeller Dawgs to provide a brief autobiography to the group. Dan was one of our few African American attendees. He'd successfully avoided my attempts to interview him, but he delivered a fine autobiography at Mack's request.

I followed along as he began to describe his family tree, starting with several generations of slaves, but the branches became tangled in my mind. According to my notes, Dan's great grandfather had been a slave who "ran away from home at nine." He "didn't consider himself either a 'house nigger' or a 'field nigger.' His identity centered around being a 'runaway.'" In addition to rebelling against subjugation, this man also taught Dan that a man never abandons his responsibilities or his family.

Apparently, at some point in the family history, Indians raided the home where his ancestors were enslaved and abducted a woman who was either his great grandmother or perhaps his great, great grandmother. It wasn't clear to me whose grandmother she'd been or how old she was when abducted. I will blame slavery for my confusion since it tends to disrupt families. Nevertheless, since slaves were valuable property, the slave owners went to the trouble of recapturing this female.

Much later, Dan's own grandmother settled in the Bronx, New York. Despite the great grandfather's teachings about family responsibility, all of Dan's uncles "got caught up in the streets and went to prison." His mother died during a back-street abortion, and his father abandoned him, so he was raised by this grandmother.

(White people put on blinders and complain that the descendants of slaves have behaved irresponsibly since slavery's abolition. However, in my humble, White opinion, it would have been very difficult for a slave to learn responsibility if he or she has no freedom to make commitments to anyone except the man holding the whip. How could the adult slave assume responsibility for relatives who could be sold, beaten, or killed at the whim of the master?)

It is remarkable to me that so few critics of policies geared to help African-Americans ask themselves, "What effect does slavery have on personality and family dynamics?" Do they think that slavery would be like being in jail, or a parent's time-out, or detention at school, as if except for being temporarily without freedom you'd be the same person with the same family, the same ideas about what you were good at, the same ambitions about your future, the same practice at planning and making decisions; and as soon as you were freed, you'd proceed with your life as a responsible, literate, knowledgeable person with a family to fall back on? If you were expected to enter white society, how would you stop feeling fear and/or hate and/or self-hate, and who would teach you to read and write, to work without being forced, to manage money, and... and...?

It isn't something my own father ever asked, and he was far from stupid. [See Chapter 17 for my short essay, "Democracy's Flaw--Part I"] In that essay, I suggest that neglect of the problems created first by slavery and then by generations of segregation, stricter in the South but present in the North too, was part of a bigger picture of indifference to the suffering of someone who is "not us." That "other" person might have a different skin color, or religion, or not live in west Texas.)

Nevertheless, Dan's grandma could take responsibility for *him*. No fool, this grandma, she saw her sons going off to jail, snatched Dan away from the stickball games out in the street, and used one uncle's GI loan and another's winnings from the numbers game to buy a home in Westchester County and move out of ghetto. Though not being of privilege or of white skin, Dan spent the rest of his childhood growing up in a privileged, White neighborhood, and he went to all-White schools since the schools weren't segregated up north. (See Brian's story.)

Upon graduation, all of his White classmates got good jobs, but he was offered none. (The jobs *were* segregated.) A friend of his father suggested he go to college. City College was free back then, so he went, graduated with a degree in architecture, moved to Harlem, and worked for projects for the city of New York. Unfortunately, the city's budget eventually went bust and they stopped paying him, so he moved to Canada, got married, and worked for the Canadians until their money ran out too. Then he finished his career in L.A. and retired to Austin.

When Dan finished his story, the Yeller Dawgs nodded in agreement. For some reason, these mostly-white Texans care about others.

Why didn't Dan tell his story to a Republican group? Not many Republicans are descendants of slaves. Not many Republicans experienced housing discrimination or job discrimination. Not many got good grades but then had trouble getting a job while paler people had no such trouble. Not many were able to achieve higher education only by living in a part of the North that would give scholarships to African-American youth. So, not many Republicans see the point to affirmative action in university enrollment or in hiring. Not many Blacks are Republicans, and few Republicans are Black, and not many Republicans care about that, so Dan attends Yeller Dawg meetings.

Chapter 10: "You're not from Texas..."[10]

Dan's autobiography was still on my mind when I sat down next to Lem at the next Yeller Dawg meeting. I was grumbling about my original question to the Yeller Dawgs: "Did the South leave the Democratic Party as a reaction against LBJ's equal rights legislation for African-Americans in the sixties?"

A big, calm-looking man, wearing a ball cap, his meaty hands folded on the table, Lem just smiled.

"Where are you from?" I asked him.

"Oklahoma," he drawled.

He grew up in a family of working people--firefighters, farmers, policemen, and the like. They didn't see the government as the enemy, and they considered themselves Democrats, with the possible exception of his mother. "She switched parties after my father died," he said.

"When was that?" I asked.

Lem paused and gazed into space, where people sometimes find memories.

"Was it soon after the passage of civil rights legislation?" I asked.

"Race may have had something to do with her switch in parties," he said, understanding my implication.

"Oklahoma's not Dixie, but it's a red state. Why aren't you a Republican?"

Lem offered a brief synopsis: "My grandfather was a Democrat and the county sheriff and a farmer too. My grandfather on my mother's side was a union man, a steelworker, a Democrat all the way."

"But that was before the civil rights legislation. Why aren't you a Republican now?"

He drawled an abstract answer: "For the middle class, one reason you vote is to determine where you want you money to go." He smiled when he added, "My grandfather was the Democratic county comptroller." Then he took the gloves off: "Do I want to give to the one percent, who will spend it where the labor is cheap, who will cheat and steal, and don't care if world ends tomorrow?"

He was giving a lot of different reasons not to vote Republican, but I still had a question: "Why didn't Civil Rights affect you the way it affected your mother?"

"My mother was smart and had huge influence on me, but she was against Civil Rights. She didn't preach racism. In her interactions with people, she

---

[10] "But Texas Wants you Anyway," Lyle Lovette

showed no prejudice, but just as it is now with Syrian refugees, people fear what they don't know. People think Muslims are all the same.

Implying, but not saying, that his mother feared Blacks, he went on to explain why he didn't fear them: "I served aboard a ship as Vietnam got underway. Some of my shipmates were Black; and I got to know them onboard ship. I saw a lot of racism in the service, and it became so abhorrent. I needed to learn as much as I could, so in college I took Psychology, child development. It might have been the Pygmalion effect.[11] If you tell a child he is smart, he will do better in school."

Lem served with African-Americans and got to know them. In this case, familiarity bred respect. It's just what a high school friend said about our playing three sports together: "We became friends. They didn't want it to happen, but they couldn't stop it."

It also reminded me of a conversation I had with a real estate appraiser in Kalamazoo, Michigan. He saw the picture of my granddaughter and asked about it.

"Yeah, she's mine," I said and waited for his response.

He smiled and confessed, "All my life I'd been sure Blacks were inferior to Whites. But when my daughter had a baby with a Black man, what could I do? Black or White, he was my grandson. I take care of him sometimes, so I've gotten to see him grow up. Now I know he's as smart and good as anyone. No one could have convinced me. It took that experience for me to know."

I told Lem, "I'll bet you don't share the views of the average White Mississippian."

"It's more ingrained in Mississippi. They are racist out of fear because the Whites are outnumbered."

"If Blacks outnumber Whites in the deep South, why isn't it Democratic?"

"If Blacks could vote, it would be Democratic."

"Why can't they? Gerrymandering?"

"After the Civil Right legislation passed, police in the South started arresting Black men and charging them with a felony. Then they'd offer them a plea bargain: 'If you admit to the felony, you will serve no jail time. The judges went along with it. A Black man facing a White sheriff, a White prosecutor, and a White jury would take the deal, so now these men can't vote because they have felonies on their records. The authorities didn't tell them that they would never be able to vote. And that is the only reason that the South has remained Republican. If it weren't for that, the South would be Democratic today. It's also

---

[11] Also called the Rosenthal effect, it's the phenomenon whereby higher expectations lead to an increase in performance.

the reason Republicans are so anti-immigration. They don't want to lose the majority."

Lem didn't want to keep the African American disenfranchised, and he didn't resent the government, not coming from a family of public servants. Neither were they beholden to corporations. Without resentment of affirmative action and desegregation, with nothing to gain from tax breaks for corporations, another issue could have turned him Republican like his mother. Rather than ask about abortion directly, I asked about his religious background.

"You know, Lem, your thinking might be unusual for a White southerner. How do you explain that? Did you attend a fundamentalist church?"

"No, Methodist. Methodists are known more as 'free thinkers' than the Baptists or evangelicals."

Lem doesn't feel obligated to dutifully follow instructions based on another person's interpretation of the Bible, not even if that man claims he's just repeating divine instructions. Roe v Wade didn't turn him Republican.

Some of Lem's message comes from how he tells his story as well as the words, themselves. He's a big man, speaks in meetings without ranting or preaching, with neither fear nor anger. Lem didn't appear to feel threatened by change, by people with dark skin, or by different ideas. He doesn't appear to feel victimized or to feel angry about mistreatment by the government due to civil rights legislation, and he showed no inclination to retaliate against anyone. Sometimes you can know a Yeller Dawg by what he isn't.

At that point, the meeting came to order and proceeded through its usual discussion of politically important issues like global warming and the usual warning against voting for Bernie Sanders, issued by one of the British members, the one who didn't think Americans would elect someone who called himself a socialist. He had a hard time selling that idea in this group, but he kept trying.

As people filed out, I began whining to Dan about the topic of racism, specifically, why at last week's meeting there was so little discussion of the continued physical intimidation or outright murder of Black Americans and so much concern about the threat ISIS posed to non-Muslim Americans. Churches were recently burned in South Carolina, threats made to black students on the U. Missouri campus.

I asked, "Are the Democrats afraid to call racism by its name, afraid to point at the campuses where it still exists--including, apparently Princeton, of all places--and afraid to call attention to the racial composition of the gerrymandered congressional districts in Red States, including Texas? Is there some reason this would be a bad strategy? What is the best way to address racism? Oddly, Obama hasn't done much about it."

(I'd already been given some answers: One reason has to do with the disenfranchisement of Black men in the South suggested by our Sooner. Another cause is gerrymandering; a third, restrictions on voting, such as a voting I.D. card which must be purchased. If Black men don't vote, supporters of Black people aren't going to get elected.)

Dan gave me an article on racism to read about why blue states have turned red.[12] The author concluded, "People on Medicaid don't vote." I don't know if he ever checked the arrest records of Black males in the formerly blue states.

---

[12]

http://www.nytimes.com/2015/11/22/opinion/sunday/who-turned-my-blue-state-red.html?emc=eta1&_r=0

Chapter 11: Speaking of Race, Where Can I Find a descendant of Mexicans?

A lot of simplistic thinking passes as political analysis. Take this example, for instance:

This interview was inspired, first, by a Yeller Dawg who argued that high minority turnout was crucial to Obama's victories in 2008 and 2012 and, second, by a high-ranking representative of the Democratic Party who reported low minority turnout in potentially Democratic portions of Texas. I wanted to talk to someone who could tell me about Mexican-American turnout. I did not know what Mexican-Americans thought about illegal immigration, so I had sought out a Mexican-American to tell me whether Texas, if it had a high minority turnout, could have any effect on the outcome of the 2016 election. Was the Republican attitude toward illegal immigration likely to drive Mexican-American voters away?

A high-ranking employee of the state Democratic party was explaining that The party would fare better if all the potential Democrats in the Houston area and in the "valley" would register and vote. My shrewd analysis of this statement began with the assumption that San Antonio lay in this "valley." I got that part right, but I still knew nothing more about the valley. My ignorance did not end there.

My next line of thought went something like this: (1) Donald Trump won a lot of support proposing a wall along the border. (2) That's simplistic. (3) I need an expert opinion. Therefore, (4) I need to talk with a Hispanic person.

The acting Chair of the Yeller Dawgs put me in touch with Carlos (not his real name. I borrowed it from the opossum we feed. He--the opossum, not the Yeller Dawg--is crunching outside the window as I type.) "Carlos" met us (me and my wife) at the Dawgs' regular haunt and I expected to get some expert testimony on the thorny problem of illegal immigration. I began with the question which has led to the title of this work:

Question: "What prevents you from voting Republican?"

Carlos: "That goes way back to my freshman year in high school when I was fourteen. I supported Richard Nixon. I was a member of the Church of Christ, which was sort of conservative, and there was all this paranoia about Kennedy being Catholic.

(Author's note: What have we learned so far? (1) Not all Mexican Americans are Catholic. (2) Not all Mexican Americans are Democrats.)

Furthermore, this particular Mexican American non-immigrant, non-Catholic Republican realized something others didn't:

At fourteen years of age, he recalls, "It occurred to me that no politician was going to let himself be perceived as being under the control of a foreign power, so I figured that Kennedy wasn't going to be a 'catholic' president, under the control of the Vatican. If he did, Americans would never elect another Catholic politician."

Carlos figured this out at fourteen, but he still favored Nixon in 1960 because he'd been steered toward conservatism since the age of ten. That was when his father told him, "That the Drew Pearson column in the paper is a very good thing to read." Carlos reported, "I read it and, yes, it was interesting." In '56 Carlos supported Eisenhower for president "because he was a general. That's all I knew, but it was enough. By time I turned fourteen in 1960, I was reading the Pearson column every day and had conservative predilections."

Then, in high school he had a debate coach who was very conservative. "She had a big influence on me," he said. "We were all conservative Republicans, thanks to her." Her conservatism fit right in in El Paso of the early sixties.

"When I started college, I was supporting Barry Goldwater, but once he was nominated, he started screwing up his campaign, starting with his acceptance speech, and it went downhill from there. I became discouraged. How can you go to Florida and say we should abolish Social Security and go to Tennessee and say the TVA should be dissolved? I was going nuts. Goldwater read Phyllis Schlafly and believed there were lots of closet conservatives out there. When he lost, I was really hurt.

"Within six months I was finishing my freshman year of college and was already a liberal democrat. After a year of college I started to develop a social conscience."

Question: "Why?"

"Because of the teachers."

Question: "Where were you in school?"

"UT-El Paso."

Question: "How did they cause the change?"

"The Poly Sci faculty, in particular, was very interested in social conscience, and the Great Society started looking better to me. My dad had raised me to be practical above all and to be honest; but while I was still in grade school, you had all these Civil Rights riots in the south, White riots against Civil Rights. My mother had really been feeling the sting of racism and sexism, and as far as she was concerned, no Black leader could say or do anything wrong. My mother had really drilled it into me. So, even in '64 while I was still a good conservative, I supported civil rights.

"As a States' Rights advocate, I saw these southerners using states rights as a justification for racial discrimination, and I thought, 'You fools, you've destroyed States' Rights by trying to use it as a shield against civil rights.' The Southerners claimed States' Rights against the anti-lynching laws. It was some time later it occurred to me that States' Rights ended in 1865 when Lee offered his sword to General Grant.

"I'm teaching a course on the presidential primaries with Lifetime Learning for Retired Citizens, and in the fall there was one conservative class member who made it clear that she was big on States' Rights. I asked her, 'Can you think of any instance when States' Rights was used for anything else other than the subjugation of African Americans?' She couldn't think of another use.

"Admittedly it had. Even opposing Obamacare, they probably threw States Rights in there, but it's mostly been used to oppose Civil Rights.

"I have to admit, I'm getting a kick out the Republicans self-destructing. With the Southern strategy [adopted by the Republican Party after LBJ's Civil Rights legislation], they sewed the seeds of their own destruction."

Question: "LBJ said, 'The Democratic Party has lost the South for fifty years."

"I think he said *thirty* years, one generation. He underestimated. They were reinforced by the Moral Majority, now the Christian Right." Confirming the underlying racism of the South's turn toward the Republican party, he reminded me, "Falwell was originally a segregationist. In 1971 he tried to pick up his tracks supporting segregation."

Question: "Your anti-racist mother had a big influence on you."

"Yes, she did, my father, too."

Question: "What is the most important issue in this election?"

"Income inequality. In my first three years I competed in extemporaneous speaking. In my final year, I was in debate; and the subject was unemployment. That was when I started learning the basics of economics."

Question: "So you won't be voting for a Texan who's supported by one percenters?"

"No."

Question: "What should we do about income equality?"

"We don't need a Republican president giving tax breaks to the rich. They aren't even earning the money. Any rich Republican has to understand that this is just a way to transfer wealth to people who aren't doing anything but gambling on the stock market. They spend a few hours per day gambling on their portfolio. It's amazing that Sanders has a receptive audience. The Democrats are sick of Wall Street guys avoiding prison. Did you see Michael Moore's film? In Iceland they locked them up."

Question: "That's Bernie Sanders' issue. What if Clinton gets the nomination?"

"Early on, certainly by end of my first year in college, my professors had made it very clear, 'Forget about voting for the man. It's the party that counts. The most liberal Republican, once he's been elected to Congress, is going to be drawn toward the Conservative side. If he or she wants to get anything done, his voting record starts sliding toward Conservatism. And a conservative Democrat, unless he or she's from the South, is going to be drawn in the liberal direction because you have to go along to get along. If you want to pass legislation to help your district so you can get re-elected, you play with the people who have the power. Even my freshman year, I heard that argument and I thought, 'That makes sense.'"

Question: "Vote the party?"

"Or don't vote at all if a conservative Democrat is running. I'm big on party discipline. I wish we had a parliamentary system. Without a parliamentary system, parties don't stand for anything. [In a two-party system, we have coalitions within parties, rather than between them.] The Republican Party has gone so far to the right that Obama drifted to the right, into the vacuum in the middle."

Question: "Unions aren't strong in the Democratic coalition now. Who's going to join the Democratic party in the future?"

"Millennials were for Obama and are now for Sanders. It's their age, connectivity and education. [He paused and smiled.] I'm an optimist."

I told him, "An official of the state Democratic party was here talking to us, and she suggested that a get out the vote campaign around San Antonio and Houston could have an effect statewide. Is it demographically possible for Texas to elect a Democrat?"

He had another wet blanket to throw on the Get-out-the-vote fire: "Lois Schlafly had the theory that with all those conservatives out there, we just had to give them a candidate conservative enough to vote for, and we'd elect conservatives. Didn't it occur to her that if nominate a candidate like that, for every Democrat you bring out to vote, you'll bring out a Republican or two? The National Democratic Party would have to pour money into Texas to get the vote out, and it's not going to waste its money on Texas right now."

Not giving up on the idea of turnout, I asked, "Not even with the big Mexican-American vote in and around San Antonio?"

"Mexicans in San Antonio are conservative. They live conservative lives, heavily influenced by the Catholic Church. More that other Catholics, Mexican-Americans observe Church teaching on abortion and birth control."

Question: "What did they think about Trump's wanting to build a wall?"

"There was a negative reaction, but a lot of Mexican-Americans like idea of a tough man, a macho man... Mexican-Americans in the Valley are now electing Mexican-American officials; but once they develop careers in business, they get more conservative. After [the age of] thirty, people start worshipping their careers because, again, 'If you want to get along, you have to go along.' Conservative politics are reinforced all the time at work."

Is he politely telling me that when I look for an ethnic Mexican to discuss Mexican immigrants, I behave like a racist too? What? I have to start thinking of Mexican-Americans as Americans?

As if he were reading my mind, he said, "I love Obama, though I didn't like his failure to prosecute the guys on Wall Street. I liked his not being a 'Black' president, like JFK wasn't as a 'Catholic' president. Catholicism isn't an issue anymore. Gene McCarthy was Catholic, but nobody cared. Americans' insecurity causes them to put people into boxes. Consciousness of race is, itself, racist."

I asked, "So how can illegal immigration be addressed?"

The very brief answer Carlos gave below had tentacles that reached back in time to NAFTA, into California's valley, west Michigan's fruit orchards, and construction projects throughout the U.S. It reminded me of my experience building a house in Texas. I took the contractor with the lowest bid, and Spanish-speaking workers poured my slab and put up my drywall. I didn't see any out-of-work Americans rushing up to grab the trowels from their hands. What can we do about illegal immigration? Carlos, who had spent the interview contradicting stereotypes about foreign, migrant workers, gave this brief answer:

"When pay goes down, immigrants go back across the border."

They come here for jobs that pay better than what they can earn at home but pay less than the wage for which Americans will work. In other words, we want inexpensive houses (like mine) and roads and food, but we complain when people sneak across the border to accept pay that Americans won't accept. Some of us complain that we've lost factory jobs, but we don't want to give up our cheap clothes and electronics. If these folks are working for wages that we won't accept, why are we complaining?

Chapter 12: Swimming Out of the Mainstream

After I announced my wish to interview Yeller Dawgs, men sat down next to me more often than women. Mack saw that the males were self-selecting as interview subjects, or women were unselecting themselves, and he called upon Amy to give a short bio about herself. It turned out that Mack's instincts were exactly right, not that Amy is a bred and born, fully pedigreed Yeller Dawg, quite the opposite. Earlier in her life would have called herself a Republican.

After her bio, she told me she initially began to attend the meetings in order to accompany her friend, who will not be interviewed because he's British, and I don't think any Englishman can rightfully be called a Yeller Dawg. Something about it just sounds wrong.

Blonde and smiling, she has a very all-American look, whatever that once meant. Looks can be deceiving: Both sides of her family claim Cherokees, and her mother was an Armenian Catholic immigrant. Somehow she came out blonde, Catholic, and Republican.

She also started life shy. In school, Amy eventually became the type of person who served as president of student organizations. And what first step did she take in her transformation? A Dale Carnegie course? A pep talk from her school counselor?

Answer: No. She underwent speech therapy. Being able to sound like everyone else when she talked lessened her self-consciousness, and made her dare to lead.

Question: But why did Amy need speech therapy?

Answer: Amy spoke with an "accent," which was due in part to listening to her immigrant mother speak.

Question: The other reason?

Answer: Her father also spoke with an unusual accent.

Question: Why?

Answer: Because he had become deaf at age seven.

As a result of her "accent," Amy was self-conscious and became something of an outsider until she learned to sound like other people, until she had a voice.

Speech therapy didn't make her a Democrat, but it informed her about the experience of being an outsider. It would come in handy with what she would be facing later in life.

Amy was raised a conservative Catholic. Despite the Cherokees on the family tree, her immediate family considered itself White and European. Her eventual political transformation would come later and was facilitated by her best friend and her first husband. Both were Hispanic. She discovered that personal connections and emotional bonds can happen outside ones ethnic and religious group. Her children provided the final push away from political conservatism.

Question: How did her two children turn her away from the Republican Party?

Answer: Her two children reminded her that not everyone is a round peg. Not everyone is the same or can be treated the same:

Amy's son was born autistic, and her daughter has an Attention Deficit Hyperactivity Disorder (ADHD). With her personal difficulty making herself understood verbally, she already knew that teachers would have difficulty knowing what to do with the differentness exhibited by her son and daughter. Services for special needs children don't simply fall into place, not even for White children from Republican families. She learned that people out of the mainstream need advocacy, allies, and accommodations for their differences. If her children were to benefit from public school, Amy would have to serve as champion and advocate with both the educational and medical systems.

Having children who weren't just like everybody else and who needed extra help and special treatment may have pushed her to a political party which sees a role for government programs. But another experience contributed.

Amy studied Business in college, but with her concern for "the little guy," she specialized in Human Resources and now serves as a consultant to government and business. She summarized, "I try to teach them to listen to their employees."

"Listening to employees" is a surprisingly revolutionary idea. It didn't spring from cotton plantations in the Southeast or from tenant farms in Texas. Its recent prominence was stimulated by an American right after World War II, but it didn't begin in America. It began in Japan.

I was growing up in Michigan in an era when Detroit's newspapers and car companies routinely shut down for employees' strikes. Disgruntled auto workers were assembling notoriously defective cars.

"Don't buy a car made on Friday," said the customer who discovered that an empty Coke bottle inside his driver's side door was causing its rattle. "On Fridays the auto workers want to get on with the weekend."

Meanwhile in Japan, a consultant named Edward Deming was telling Japanese auto execs they should listen to their employees and reduce their fear of failure and job loss. Hierarchical, top-down management in Detroit didn't like this philosophy and rejected it. When the 1970's rolled around, Japan was producing cars of higher quality than Detroit's,[13] and Hondas and Toyotas were stealing market share from the Big Three.

This culture of listening to employees has since caught on and may currently be epitomized by Zingerman's of Ann Arbor, which one consultant described as follows: "At Zingerman's each employee is thought of as a customer whose satisfaction is crucial to the success of the company. A disgruntled employee is going to leave disgruntled customers in his or her wake."

The philosophy is that an unhappy employee is not going to make a good corned beef sandwich or leave the customer happy, and customer service has made Zingerman's various businesses successful. Listening to what other people think and feel works best if the listener actually cares what others think and feel. When some people seem to be listening, they are really only waiting till you stop talking so they can tell you what to think. Lots of business executives function in that way, and it leads to dysfunction in their employees and bad performance by the organization. This is the kind of thing formerly voiceless Amy endeavors to teach business managers and owners.

Thus, Amy came to understand the importance of listening--always an issue for the girl whose father couldn't hear, who needed therapy to make herself understood, who later had to speak up to make herself heard so doctors and teachers could understand her children. Amy now tries to spread the message to others.

Listening: that is what Amy learned how to do and teaches others, not what to think, not to judge, but how to listen, "to lift the fallen, to restore the broken, and to heal the hurting."

It is difficult message for business executive to accept, and the "why" is obvious. First, it isn't his job to lift the fallen. His job is to make the biggest profit possible. Business owners do not by nature want really free markets. They want to maximize profits; and to do that, they would like a market they could control. That is because though competition is the fuel of a market, it is the enemy of profit. Free markets encourage competition and threaten a business' security and profits. Republicans say they want markets free of government interference, but

---

[13] per Wikipedia (Deming, Edward) In the 1970s, Deming's philosophy was summarized by some of his Japanese proponents with the following 'a'-versus-'b' comparison:

    (a) When people and organizations focus primarily on quality, quality tends to increase and costs fall over time.

    (b) However, when people and organizations focus primarily on *costs*, costs tend to rise and quality declines over time.

historically government has had to interfere in order to keep markets functioning correctly and free from price fixing.[14]

In the 1800s, there were several giant businesses known as "trusts." Without competition, prices went through the roof and quality didn't have to be a business' priority. The Sherman Act is the nation's oldest antitrust law. Passed in 1890 and signed by Republican Benjamin Harrison, it makes it illegal for competitors to make agreements with each other that would limit competition. So, for example, they can't agree to set a high price for a product—that would be price fixing.

With the Federal Trade Commission (FTC) Act (1914), Congress created a new federal agency to watch out for unfair business practices—and gave the FTC the authority to investigate and stop unfair methods of competition and deceptive practices. Theodore Roosevelt did a couple of things that wouldn't win the approval of any current Republican. He "busted" many trusts by enforcing what came to be known as "antitrust" laws. The goal of these laws was to protect consumers by promoting competition in the marketplace. He not only busted up trusts, he also championed the National Park system, including its restrictions on mining and drilling.

So there are different ways to be a Republican. A Teddy Roosevelt Republican will use government power to keep markets functioning as the economists envisioned. In our current world, can we trust oil companies to give us the cheapest, cleanest energy possible? Their job isn't to save the consumer's money or keep the ice caps frozen. Their job is to maximize profit. Why would the average person want them in charge?

With all of this as background, it is interesting that Yeller Dawg Amy tries to teach business owners and government officials how to be more successful by listening and being less authoritarian. I suspect it works best in enterprises which have little control over markets and need to appeal to customers to win their business from the competition, not like the Big Three automakers of the 1970's.

---

[14]
(http://www.consumer.ftc.gov/sites/default/files/games/off-site/youarehere/pages/pdf/FTC-Competition_Antitrust-Laws.pdf)

Chapter 13: Two former Republicans in Search of Fiscal Responsibility

Amy left the Republicans as she began to champion people whose needs required attention. In addition to her, I found two former Republican who deserted their former party looking for fiscal responsibility.

I found the first when I sat down next to one of the Yeller Dawgs who'd attended almost every meeting since my arrival. I asked him why he couldn't vote Republican and thought of Amy when he answered, "I used to vote Republican as often as I voted Democrat. I appreciated their fiscal conservatism, even though Reagan didn't practice what he preached. (Reagan presided over the biggest budget deficits the nation had ever seen. His Vice President, George Bush I, always considered Reagan to preach 'voodoo economics' and raised taxes to balance the budget. He probably lost to Clinton for his trouble. Bush II then cut taxes and resumed the budget deficits that had disappeared during the Clinton administration.

"So," he said, "I didn't leave them. They left me. This current batch makes no sense. They've sold out to the Gun lobby, to big corporations, and to the religious right. They aren't looking out for the country." The meeting started, and we never got back to what he was telling me.

Former Republican #2, Darin, was also able to vote Republican in the past. In fact, he considered himself a Republican until the 80's, a Rockefeller Republican, i.e., a financial conservative but socially liberal. He told me, "In the 80's the party was taken over by right wing Christians. I think that was Carl Rove's idea, that, plus the racists that had been Democrats, Dixiecrats, really. The reasonable Republicans have left. Now, Democrats are fiscally more responsible than the Republicans."

Chapter 14: Another Case of Changing Parties

Like the two Yeller Dawgs mentioned above, Marcia spent most of her life as a Republican. Born shortly before World War II, she was just two years of age when her father died, and she found herself as the only daughter to a Virginia schoolteacher. When the U.S. entered the war, her mother joined the Red Cross; and Marcia went to live with her grandparents. Her life in a Republican family proceeded through college, where she majored in dietetics. Loving courses like Philosophy and Psychology, she found herself studying Organic Chemistry instead.

"It was the wrong career for me," she said. "I never liked to cook. I probably did it because someone told me that 'the way to a man's heart is through his stomach.'"

A few years after graduating, she did find her way to a man's heart, got married, and gave birth to a baby girl. She moved west to Texas with her new family and began to meet regularly with a group of Republican women in her new hometown. When I asked her about the appeal of the Republican party, she, like the convert quoted in the previous chapter, cited "its fiscal conservatism."

But she wasn't giving politics much thought at all, if the truth be told. She said she'd been a lifelong Republican and joined the Republican women's group "for social reasons." Her friends were Republican, "and it was because of money." When asked about the attitudes of the membership, she said, "They didn't like the handouts" (provided by the Democrats after LBJ)... One woman came from Poland and married an American soldier. She used to say, 'These bums on the street, they ought to go out and get a job,' but not everybody can go out and get a job. I kept telling her things like, 'In Germany a new mother will get paid leave for whatever time she needs.' She was a nice lady, but she thought too much about handouts. It's the money thing. She lacks sympathy for the poor." Turning psychologist, she suggested, "I don't think they want to be identified with the poor. Being a Republican has a lot to do with money, don't you think?"

(She was asking the wrong guy. That's what I was trying to figure out.)

But soon thereafter, at a friend's birthday party, a fellow writer asked about the current book project--this one--and I told him the title. He said that as a young woman his mother had worked for the head of a state Republican party and was going to register to vote.

"Which party?" the Republican boss asked.

"Republican, of course," she answered.

"Don't do that," he told her. "This is not the party for you. This party was built to increase the wealth of the wealthy. That's who it serves. It doesn't serve your interests."

I thanked the storyteller and offered him a footnote, but he said it wasn't necessary.)[15]

Marcia soon stopped attending the Republican women's meetings, but not for fiscal reasons. Not wealthy but never indigent, Marcia felt at home in a women's group that didn't believe anybody really needed food stamps or LBJ's disastrous Aid to Dependent Children (which helped fill schools with fatherless children until repealed under Clinton.)

The GOP didn't lose Marcia because George W. Bush did away with the Clinton budget surpluses by invading two Middle Eastern countries--one (Afghanistan) in search of Osama Bin Laden, but the other (Iraq), in search of who knows what--and at the same time cut taxes for the wealthy, thereby running up the national debt.

No, Marcia was bothered by the loss of life more than the loss of treasure: "Bush II and his war made me a Democrat. I learned that we should stay out of war. World War II was the last necessary war. I'm a peace activist now. We shouldn't get mixed up in Middle East. It's run by clans. They don't want democracy."

When George W. Bush convinced the Congress and most of the nation that the armed forces needed to invade Iraq to rid them of imaginary weapons of mass destruction, she became a self-described peace activist, and she stopped voting Republican, not out of political ideology, but because of her moral revulsion over killing and dying for no reason that made any sense to her.

Now a critic of politicians, she slid a copy of *Saving Capitalism* across the coffee-house's table, saying, "I believe in structured capitalism." This sounded more like economist/Yeller-Dawg-founder Woodrow than the member of a Republican Women's Group.

Currently helping her granddaughter finance college, she asked me, "Did you know that the bankruptcy code doesn't apply to student loans? Your pay can

---

[15] That same day, another writer-friend described a poster of a decrepit old man, wearing a sixty year-old Confederate uniform and snarling, 'Forget? Never!' That old soldier's long-gone now, but his descendants still remember the fight against secession and its underlying cause, slavery, as well as the ultimate insult to the inheritors of the confederacy, vis., LBJ"s civil rights legislation.

be garnisheed." Next she said something that at first seemed unrelated, "That's one reason I like Canada: Their banks are regulated. They didn't have a crash in '08."

She went on about Canada, "I had nice neighbors. She was a schoolteacher. When Texas passed the open-carry gun law, they moved to Oregon. They have gun control in Canada. Canada has a single-payer health plan. Here, insurance companies make out like bandits. A friend of mine buys drugs from Canada because they're cheaper. In Canada they look out more for the little guy.

"In Canada, a particular immigrant was ranting like a Nazi. He was warned but kept it up, so they deported him, not like here where some Baptists, I think it was, traveled a thousand miles to the funeral of a gay soldier and screamed, 'You're a faggot! God hates you!'"

"I think the Democrats look out more for the little guy. My father and uncles weren't concerned with people who had less. I think Democrats are."

It was hard at first to know where she was headed when she said, "I've been thinking about Warren Buffett. I read an article that he lives kind of modestly. That's interesting. He said he pays a lower tax rate than his secretary." But this life-long Republican was still on message: "People vote Republican because the Republican Party is the money party, and that's what they want more of."

Now it all made sense--the wars, the health care, the student loans: It's all about money.

Chapter 15: Poet Laureate of the Yeller Dawgs

Around the fourth of July, it might have been, Dylan showed up dressed as Benjamin Franklin and gave a speech about our nation's founding, but I hadn't started this project yet, so I didn't record it. Later, as the Iowa caucuses were voting, he announced a march on Washington to marshal support for a constitutional amendment that would nullify the Supreme Court's Citizens United decision. Being a lawyer as well as a Ben Franklin impersonator, he explained the legal history of the concept that a corporation has the rights of a person.

In 1886 the U.S. Supreme Court heard a case between Santa Clara County and the Southern Pacific Railroad, which were disputing a rail bed route. In its decision the Court ruled "that a private corporation was a 'natural person' under the US Constitution and therefore entitled to protection under the Bill of Rights. Suddenly, corporations enjoyed all the rights and sovereignty previously enjoyed only by the people, including the right to free speech. This 1886 decision ostensibly gave corporations the same powers as private citizens. But considering their vast financial resources, corporations thereafter actually had far more power than any private citizen."[16]

Apparently, the Roberts Court based its Citizens United decision on this precedent; and Dylan told us, "If the constitution cannot be amended to nullify Citizen's United, the richest one percent will run the country."

That caught my attention. Curious about his Ben Franklin costume, I continued reading about the status of corporations in Franklin's day. One source argued that the "colonists... feared... chartered entities" such as the "Massachusetts Bay Company, the Hudson's Bay Company, the British East India Company... They recognized the way British kings and their cronies used them as robotic arms to control the affairs of the colonies, to pinch staples from remote breadbaskets and bring them home to the motherland."[17]

In addition, the corporation was seen as an ally of the British government in imposing duties on goods such as the tea that sparked the Boston Tea Party and the American Revolution. Those early colonists wouldn't have wanted corporations, or at least British corporations, to have full civil rights.

In this view, "The Declaration of Independence, in 1776, freed Americans not only from Britain but also from the tyranny of British corporations, and for a

---

[16] https://en.wikipedia.org/wiki/Santa_Clara_County_v._Southern_Pacific_Railroad_Co.
[17] *Adbusters*, 28-32, P. 52

hundred years after the document's signing, Americans remained deeply suspicious of corporate power. They were careful about the way they granted corporate charters, and about the powers granted therein.

"Early American charters were created literally by the people, for the people as a legal convenience. Corporations were 'artificial, invisible, intangible,' mere financial tools. They were chartered by individual states, not the federal government, which meant they could be kept under close local scrutiny. They were automatically dissolved if they engaged in activities that violated their charter. Limits were placed on how big and powerful companies could become. Even railroad magnate J. P. Morgan, the consummate capitalist, understood that corporations must never become so big that they "inhibit freedom to the point where efficiency [is] endangered."[18]

Apparently, some corporations got rich and grew in power during and after the Civil War. Lincoln foresaw terrible trouble. Shortly before his death, he warned that "corporations have been enthroned . . . . An era of corruption in high places will follow and the money power will endeavor to prolong its reign by working on the prejudices of the people . . . until wealth is aggregated in a few hands . . . and the republic is destroyed."[19]

Some of the hands holding onto considerable profits as the Civil War was ending belonged to bankers. Lincoln reportedly said, "The money powers prey upon the nation in times of peace and conspire against it in times of adversity. The banking powers are more despotic than a monarchy, more insolent than autocracy, more selfish than bureaucracy. They denounce as public enemies all who question their methods or throw light upon their crimes. I have two great enemies, the Southern Army in front of me and the bankers in the rear. Of the two, the one at my rear is my greatest foe."[20]

Less surprisingly, trust-busting Theodore Roosevelt said, "We must drive the special interests out of politics. The citizens of the United States must effectively control the mighty commercial forces which they have themselves called into being. There can be no effective control of corporations while their political activity remains."[21]

I reminded Dylan that 1886 was about the time Robber Baron Jay Gould bragged how he broke up a strike of railroad workers in Georgia: "I can hire half

---

[18] Adbusters, editions 28-32

[19] http://www.ratical.org/corporations/Lincoln.html

[20]

http://www.opednews.com/Quotations/The-money-powers-prey-upon-the-by-Lincoln-Abraham-111016-448.html

[21] https://en.wikipedia.org/wiki/Political_positions_of_Theodore_Roosevelt

the working class to kill the other half."[22] I wondered how he came about this Lincoln-Roosevelt type of Republican point of view. At my request he wrote the following:

"My relatives were working folks. Both grandfathers and my Dad worked for the Texas & Pacific Railroad in Longview, Texas. Although none of my grandparents were active in national politics, I recall one or another of them many times saying around the dinner table, "Don't ever vote for a Republican because they will bring on another Depression." In those days in East Texas, the Republican Party didn't exist.

"I have lived in Austin since September, 1959, when I enrolled at UT. I graduated from Law School in 1964, have an undergraduate degree in Government (now called Political Science). I was a precinct worker and heard John F. Kennedy speak at the State Capitol when he was campaigning for President in 1960. Very inspirational.

"I worked as campaign chairman for a State Rep ... in 19... and ran for State Representative in Austin as a Democrat in..., finishing third .... (Until you run, you cannot understand what running for office entails).

"I have been a Board-Certified trial attorney since ... I served as ... Assistant Attorney General, State of ..., in the administration of ... from 19... to 19... I am also a Mediator.

"I have written, produced and acted in two short presentations: ... *Defend The Constitution* (in response to G.W. Bush's statement, 'The Constitution is nothing but a damn piece of paper,' and *[another]* after Citizens United was decided).

"I became a Yeller Dawg after the U.S. Supreme Court declared George Bush President in 2000 while the recount was still underway in Florida. After Bush won on a platform of "Family Values," I started to study politics in depth to understand how an idiot like Bush could become President. Those studies continue.

"I love the spirit and spunk of the Yeller Dawgs. In addition to 'cussin' and discussin' matters of the day at the Dawgs meetings, I have served (until February, 2015) as the Chair of the Messaging Committee, Travis County Democratic Party and precinct chairman, each for two years. I am currently working with Public Citizen, Moveon.org, and other .orgs in organizing the Democracy Awakening movement which will come to fruition this April in Washington, D.C. Our aim is to pass a Constitutional Amendment to overturn Citizens United--16 State Legislatures have so far passed resolutions urging

---

[22] Reames, Hal, "To Kill the Other Half," 2014.

Congress to put such an Amendment before the people, and we are working to get the 2/3 majority to do so."

Along with his duties as Ben Franklin impersonator, Dylan's labors as poet laureate of the Yeller Dawgs have produced two musical works, including this:

A MODEST TRIBUTE TO "Woodrow Knoll" YELLER DAWG LAUREATE

Gentle of voice but firm of mind,
The Yeller Dawgs of Texas made a great find.
Our teacher, our friend, a political Devine,
Nuggets of knowledge, he did mine.
A professor, he wanted to be, Thirsting for knowledge, you see. "You shall know the truth and it will set you free."
Professor Emeritus at U.T. Imparting knowledge to students, his special gift,
Never preaching, never pontificating, making no rift.
Just planting good seeds in fertile minds,
Always ahead, never behind, the times.
Like Bedicheck, Dobie and Webb, a country boy,
Enriched young minds, with great joy.
Now our poet, our Shakespeare, our muse,
Pick the word most applicable, as you choose.
Now you are our teacher, our friend our Devine,
A Yeller Dawg forever, what a great find !
Oh be gentle with us great Oracle, as you speak,
Our spirits are willing but our minds are weak.
Banking and economics we understand not a whit,
Corporations, plutocrats and lobbyists make us spit.
Give us a chance and we will someday see,
Glimmers of light that you already see.

Presented on behalf of the Yeller Dawgs of Texas, To our great friend, Woodrow Knoll, on May 14, 2011. Xxxxxxx

He also composed, and may have sung, the "Yeller Dawgs of Texas"[23] (to the tune of "Yellow Rose of Texas.")

---

[23] Names have been changed to protect the Dawgs

Chapter 16: Son of an Immigrant

In addition to writing a college textbook, Jacob has published his own memoir, which contains many personal insights and poses a very interesting hypothesis about the unconscious mind. All of that work contributes to an understanding of his attitudes, values, and politics, but much of it exceeds the scope of the political leanings of Texans. From his life story I have extracted a number of highlights.

Born in Detroit in 1943, he was the only child living under the watchful eyes of seven Jewish, immigrant adults, including his parents. After telling how physically intimidating his father's intensity could be to man and boy alike, he explained, "My father was also very judgmental, and his condemnations of my behavior followed me well into adulthood. I know I disappointed him in the kind of boy I was. He wanted me to be tough like him, to excel in sports, to be hyper-masculine and not show my feelings. But instead, I was emotionally timid and scared of many things, just like my mother."

From the beginning, Jacob never could follow in his father's footsteps. Then, at the age of thirteen, he began exhibiting the symptoms of ulcerative colitis, a painful disease which interfered with his growth and physical development, his physical activity, his confidence, and his social life. In young adulthood, the colon was removed, and he began wearing a colostomy bag.

Suffice it to say, Jacob was not given any of the ingredients one might need to vote Republican in Texas. Though having a powerful (i.e., intimidating) father, he was not, himself, economically or politically powerful; and given the differences between a teenager handicapped by colitis and his physically strong and aggressive father, Jacob wasn't inclined to follow in the his father's footsteps.

Regardless, he doesn't mention politics as interesting or important to him or his family as he grew up. There was no family ideology to follow. The family was Jewish, but they certainly did not consider the stories of the Old Testament to be literally true or to serve as instructions to forbid abortions and gay marriage or to ignore the environment.

Rather than focusing on external enemies, such as welfare recipients, union members, blacks, tax collectors, or people trying to take away his guns (of which he had none), he was more drawn to a rabbi and sociology professor at the university he attended. He described the man as "smart..., articulate, kind, and an excellent teacher." These traits he valued.

Jewish and physically handicapped to a degree, Jacob didn't find a place in a largely Christian, adolescent subculture. He had suffered both physically and emotionally growing up; and the professor was someone with whom he could identify. Not aspiring to wealth or power, not threatened by sharing a drinking fountain or seat on a bus with an African-American, not adhering to the doctrine that free markets will solve all problems, he didn't oppose helping hourly wage-earners by legalizing unions or taxing corporations or their wealthy. Not believing in the literal interpretation of those parts of the Torah that became the Old Testament, he didn't object to women having abortions or gays getting married. An author, clinician, and educator, Jacob didn't think all of life's important questions had been answered, and he didn't stop learning.

In a previous chapter, Marcia said that Democrats care more about the "little guy." Physically handicapped and financially limited early in life, Jacob was not one of the rich and powerful and didn't yearn to be. He valued intelligence, knowledge, and compassion, so he learned how to help people with emotional problems and, in particular, turned his attention to other minorities. Finding nothing in common with Republicans, he became first a healer and later a Yeller Dawg.

Chapter 17: A Man Who Sees Things Differently

Early in my attendance at Yeller Dawg meetings, I read them a little vignette called "Democracy's Flaw--Part I", which I'd written to explain my confusion about Republicans:

Plato argued that democracy can't work because the common man would be persuaded by demagogues, but that's not right. There is another reason. Take my father, for example:

He grew up during the Great Depression, and his own father died young of tuberculosis. Without money, he still managed to earn an M.D. and then a PhD., so he was a smart man, but did he understand the concept of a nation? Did he understand when a nation should address a problem?

When the Surgeon General of the United States first announced that cigarette smoke was implicated in lung cancer, did my physician father quit smoking? Did he even stop smoking while driving his family in a closed car? Of course not. But why not? Did stupidity make him listen to Philip Morris' denials?

Did he stop buying aerosol sprays after a lab experiment suggested that hydrofluorocarbons could deplete the Ozone layer? If anyone should've understood the implications of that study, it should have been my M.D., Ph.D. father, but when I fretted about buying spray deodorants, he advised, "Don't worry, Earth is a big planet. There won't be any holes in the Ozone layer." He died in 1993 as I was in-flight to Auckland, New Zealand, which sat right under an ozone hole and had the highest skin cancer rate in the world.

Earth might be a big place, as he said, but my father lived in a small world and suffered from the flaw of conservatism: I never heard him say that anything should be different from the way it was--not smoking, not poverty, not the VietNam War, and not racism.

As far as he was concerned, we didn't live in a segregated city. To him, the all-black north side of our town was another community, an unfortunate community, but not his concern. He remained passive like George Bush after hurricane Katrina devastated New Orleans.

If my home had been washed away by a tropical storm, my father would have helped, but Bush did little to aid the storm victims. Visiting New Orleans, a different president scolded us for failing to nourish our communities. By calling them "our" communities, he took an unselfish, non-conservative position, not my father's position.

During the Depression, my father's mind was nourished because a wealthy banker saw him as part of his community and loaned him money. I loved my father, but he wouldn't have cared enough to loan money to a promising child in Louisiana. My father would never have understood that rich German businessman who defended his country's 55% tax rate, saying: "I like being rich, but I don't want to live in a poor country."

My country seemed to grow a heart briefly during the Great Depression when most people were dirt poor. Then we understood that poverty isn't always the result of laziness, and hard work sometimes isn't enough, and we were briefly a community, and my father benefitted but then forgot why."

I decided to broaden my search for an answer and planned to attend another meeting that attracted Yeller Dawg types, but I arrived five or ten minutes late for the meeting, so I was surprised to find Andy standing outside, apparently leaving.

(It turned out that the meeting had already ended. Being a psychologist, I figured my confusion about the meeting time must have been the result of mixed feelings about supporting a Democrat. I'd first considered myself a Democrat when LBJ ran against Barry Goldwater, congratulated myself after the Civil Rights legislation was passed in the '60's, doubted my judgement when The Great Society began paying women to have fatherless babies; and after Johnson started drafting guys my age into the Vietnam war, I fled from the Democrats for the next fifty years.)

Andy smiled through a graying beard and announced, "Hey, I've been wanting to talk to you about your Daddy issues."

"I didn't have a problem with my father," I protested. "I am just trying to understand why he was a Republican and the Yeller Dawgs aren't.'

"Let's have lunch some time," he said.

I found Andy waiting in what was, according to one yearly poll, "Austin's best taco bar." In Austin an expensive decor that raises the price of a taco adds nothing to the rating of the restaurant. Only the food matters. Austin is proudly weird.

At that meeting he gave me some books to read, including *The Populist Moment--A short History of the Agrarian Revolt in America,* by Lawrence Goodwyn. Andy was making me think. I had, for all practical purposes, forgotten what farmers in previous generations had endured when families like

Woodrow's lived on credit, borrowing more for each crop, and growing deeper and deeper in debt each season, never making enough to get out of debt.

Farmers in the Grange movement briefly escaped the clutches of the bankers and suppliers, not through the vote, but by sending their business to cooperative stores. The Populist theory was good, but those who were benefitting from and controlling the system already in place had nothing to gain from change. Thus, commercial institutions united against the Populists--the Chicago stockyards, grain elevator companies, railroads, mortgage companies, merchants. The Populists fell short of gaining control of a major party, and they couldn't persuade southeastern farmers or northern factory workers to abandon their party affiliations for a third party.

In Andy's view, the populism of the late nineteenth century Grange movement was a fleeting opportunity for people at the grassroots to unite, cooperate, and wrest control of farming and manufacturing from the bankers and financiers. According to him, it died after 1896 under the weight of the Republicans' ability to finance campaigns.

"The corporate state emerged." As a result, says Andy, "Control of money stayed in the hands of commercial banks and the selective vision of the wealthy... This is the key: They had no way to bypass the monopolies, banks...

"People don't just decide it would be a good time to change. They change when they must, and the time is coming. We're headed for a collapse because decisions are not being made *by* the people, but *for* the people by a global power structure that distributes resources and determines what we eat and wear, and it's all based on a mirage, the value of money or stocks or oil."

In other words, he meant, "Once we lose faith in the value of currency, it all collapses." I asked why it would all collapse.

Andy argued that our selfish and competitive, adversarial approach to problems and solutions has taken us to the brink. Unions were once a counterbalance against the power of big business. They seem to have gone out of fashion lately, and I wondered how many people remember what kind of wage factory workers, miners, seamstresses, etc. earned before unions gained power. No one has been alive long enough to remember the power held by corporations before Theodore Roosevelt signed the anti-trust laws, back when Robber Baron Jay Gould proudly bragged, "I can hire half the working class to kill the other half."

Andy earned a Master's in political science, meaning he'd written up some original research. He brought a copy with him along with the book about populism. I'd earned a Masters in Psychology with a little, ten-page journal article, but Andy slid a tome between the tacos. "Here, you can borrow a copy of my thesis."

As I later found out, his research concerned how members of a city council formed alliances with one another. At this point, though, I didn't see the connection between Andy's research and his membership in the Yeller Dawgs.

It turns out that the politicians he was studying didn't vote strictly according to where they fell on the political spectrum. In other words, the far left didn't always vote with the near left, and the far right didn't necessarily vote with the near right. The finding that moderate right and moderate left sometimes voted together didn't come as a surprise, but the frequency with which far right and far left voted together wasn't expected and lay at the heart of his thesis. He proposed that people at the opposite ends of the spectrum often processed information in similar ways and shared a view of how decisions should be made. Sometimes they voted with people who processed information similarly to them, for example, those who took people's feelings into consideration in making decisions.

Sometimes interesting research findings such as this escapes notice. Sometimes one must look at things from a different perspective to see something new. Questions sprung to my mind: Why would political scientist Andy notice such a tendency in voting patterns? Why would Andy pay attention to how people out of the mainstream might process information?

When I asked Andy how he had come to develop his non-Republican voting pattern while living in Republican Texas, he explained two reasons why he seemed to diverge from the mainstream. First, he immigrated to Texas and arrived in Dallas with a northern accent, which made him sound different. But there was something else, something more important: He is a self-described "dyslexic." He wasn't saying he hadn't learned to read. Judging from the size of his Master's thesis, he'd mastered writing as well as reading. He explained, "I've always processed information differently than most people do. I grew up in racist, xenophobic Dallas where I was the outsider with dyslexia. I didn't connect like everybody else. I didn't know when others would be coming at me. Those experiences make you... less confident of your safety, less sure you know the right answers."

The second finding of his thesis concerned another difference between people on the fringes and those toward the center. His study found that those on the extreme had a more grassroots approach to governance and a lesser inclination to follow those in authority. Judging from Andy's comments at Yeller Dawgs meetings, he shares these traits one finds at the political extremes. Thus, he is not inclined to support a candidate just because he or she appeals to those in power, i.e., to the party bosses or the political leaders.

Conventional wisdom is not sacred to this guy. He isn't going to trust in a top-down power structure. Rather than assume power, he would prefer to empower the citizen. He is not a born or bred follower, not a believer in the wisdom of the status quo, not a trusting follower of the elite, the powerful, or the pastor, and he is not a Republican.

A week or so later, at my second meeting with Andy, I told him, "I've paged through the books you gave me, but I've spent most of my time on your thesis. I don't remember anyone else calling attention to tendencies in the personality affecting political coalitions, except for those who talk about finding personality types at certain parts of the political spectrum (like the high F scale authoritarian, currently most common on the Right in our country). The feeling-oriented, maybe right-brained, Progressive is certainly distinct from the selfish (and also logical), Republican father I described in my story.

"So, I find my curiosity about the Yeller Dawgs piqued. It's not a homogeneous group, and I have no desire to homogenize it by looking for common denominators. I wonder if some are driven by compassion for the under-served, some intellectually offended by the flaws of U.S. capitalism."

Andy responded unexpectedly, "We approach politics like consumers."

I didn't know exactly what that meant. He seemed to have changed the subject.

He went on, "A joke I tell at Yeller Dawgs is that 'We lose the war but live to fight another battle.'" He argues that the Yeller Dawgs address policy but not the structure of decision-making. "My politics would be to change people through their experience. I think that's how communities are moved..., not by some intellectual notion that they have consumed..."

He sees most people as thinking very little to reach an understanding about the issues, but instead just choosing which side they are on, like Republicans or like Democrats. He sees the voter as sleepwalking in the direction set by leaders. Instead he says, "I'm proposing a tribal structure based on our hard-wiring. Right now, our choice of relationship to power is limited to being either the ally or the victim of those who hold power. The voter who doesn't support the winner loses his voice."

Andy imagines that everybody can potentially function as a leader at some level of government, but he fears that the 1%'ers can limit popular sovereignty by limiting education. His only hope for a new structure lies in a populist system in which people don't just elect people to make policy but shape policy through ongoing local, town-meeting-like activities which inform and direct elected officials.

Andy's view of political decision-making led me to ask, "Can a nation currently home to 330 million people be governed by town meetings? Do people even want the responsibility?"

He acknowledged, "There are lots of reasons to be depressed." He said he has mixed feelings about his own ideas: "I've always suffered from both inferiority and superiority complexes," stemming, one might guess, from seeing pervasive structural problems but doubting that solutions which make sense in the abstract can really work in reality.

He suggested that revolutionary change requires that most voters must perceive the established system as broken. Andy wasn't convinced they did. Thus, though he didn't criticize Republican positions, they didn't appeal to him. He just saw them as perhaps a little more closely tied to the banks and oil companies than those of the Democrats.

When I tried to place current presidential candidates in one of Andy's four groups, I had trouble placing Hillary firmly in either "liberal" or "conservative." I then asked why he preferred Sanders over her.

He answered, "Clinton doesn't have the skill-set to deal with the chaos that will follow the coming collapse. She's more closely tied to Wall Street. Sanders is more of a Populist."

The Yeller Dawgs are more on the fringe than the centrist Democrats. Andy finds common ground on the edges, on the fringe.

Chapter 18: Education and Reason

I sat down next to JW at my very first Yeller Dawg meeting. As the lunches were being passed around, I leaned over and asked him why he wasn't a Republican. He answered, "Because the Democrats don't usually screw things up as badly as the Republicans."

Later, when I began asking that question to other Dawgs, I approached JW again, now with my recorder in hand, but he hurried away, explaining, "My wife has Alzheimer's and I can't leave her alone for long."

JW didn't pull his punches.

When we had a minute at a subsequent meeting, I asked about her, but he didn't have any good news to report, not with Alzheimer's, so I asked how he happened to become a schoolteacher in Austin. He got right to the point: "Education is the key to a good life. I was a native Detroiter. I had to drop out of school to contribute to the family income so my sister could finish high school and then college. From the age of 10 to 18 I sold papers. I went back to school but entered the Air Corps in 1943 during WWII and went to Massachusetts and learned how to fly B-52's.

"My sister had become a secretary and office manager, and she sent me the information I needed to finish high school by doing an extension course while stationed in China.

"After the war, I got married. My wife had graduated from nursing school in 1944. We settled in Austin where we had three children. One is a writer. Another is a Professor at U. T., and the third is an engineer for NASA.

"I finished my education with a B.S. in Social Sciences and an M.A. in Government, (both with honors) and taught school in Austin from 1968 to '88, encouraging my students to learn how to think, to continue their education, and to use reason."

So when JW stands up to address his fellow Dawgs, he doesn't tell us what the government should do for people. As a brother, soldier, husband, and father, he had taken on the job of caring for his own people. At the Yeller Dawg meetings, he doesn't preach hand-outs. Instead, he gives us a history lesson and urges us not to repeat past mistakes, encouraging us to think rationally, usually advising against military involvement in foreign lands with different cultures. Dedicated to knowledge and reason, he is not likely to support national politicians who vote in favor invading Iraq or Syria without a clear and achievable goal.

If he had been sitting next to me at the lecture about the likelihood of serious droughts in the future and heard that our state politicians voted against improved drought planning because the Bible didn't tell them to worry about it, he would've shaken his head in disbelief. After all, he had taught his students "to think, to continue their education, and to use reason."

Chapter 19: Thresholds and Beyond

By guest contributor, Vern

"The cumulative effect of recent world events on my psyche produced enough incentive to write yet another summary of the human condition as I see it, and imagine what the pathway to the future looks like." He quotes Rebecca Costa, author of *The Watchman's Rattle*, to cite biologist E.O. Wilson: "The real problem of humanity is the following: We have Paleolithic emotions, medieval institutions and god-like technology."

Then he turns to the collapse of the Mayan civilization to explain how civilizations have disappeared when they faced a problem for which they had no solution; and rather than think innovatively to come up with actual solutions, they trusted in their belief systems:

"The paradox is illustrated in various ancient civilizations that failed, and they all failed for the same reasons and in the same way. Ancient civilizations performed marvelous feats of ingenuity and engineering to survive and thrive under certain, given conditions. The Mayans, for example built enormous, elaborate irrigation and water conservation structures that allowed for irrigation and farming to support populations numbering in the millions. Sadly, though, their work was designed for the 'normal' conditions under which they thrived. Geological records, however, show a sustained period of drought of which the Mayans could not engineer their way out. So, instead of working toward new ways to preserve their way of life, they reached a cognitive threshold where they either couldn't or wouldn't make the necessary decisions to solve the coming problem. This period of gridlock is known as the *cognitive threshold.*

"Upon reaching this threshold, the Mayans reverted to their belief system of deities and rituals to work their way out of the problem; they substituted beliefs for real solutions. Human and animal sacrifices took the place of engineering projects and group efforts to overcome the shrinking water supply. Instead of building more cisterns, they killed more virgins... History also shows that societies advance quickly and thrive when their beliefs AND knowledge work side-by-side to satisfy the human needs necessary...

"Thom Hartmann's book, The Crash of 2016 is another chilling survey of our particular situation in the United States and the world in which we live. The pattern for the previous three crashes began with government gridlock followed by an economic meltdown, followed by a terrible war, followed by major reformation... The patterns defined by Costa and Hartmann have some things in common, namely gridlock (cognitive threshold) followed by the passing on of problems and increasing complexity to subsequent generations to solve. Except they don't get solved."

With this foundation he arrives at our current situation: "The resurgence of religious beliefs in our political discourse is a recapitulation of the Mayan collapse. Ted Cruz, for example, trots out his father who says he hears God's voice telling him his son MUST become President of the United States. Now, rational people get it that this stuff gets most people into padded rooms and fed soft food, but Ted gets funded by the Koch brothers who have a reformation of their own in mind: A free-market, theological oligarchy. That mouthful of words really describes the ultimate outcome for suspended problem solving in that it completely ignores all of history, the Constitution, and how democratic economics work... It is a total suspension of anything but beliefs of a system that has been proven over and over to *not* work.

It is worth repeating the argument that won the hearts of the Texas legislature: "God put the Earth here to take care of us. He didn't put us here to take care of the Earth."

And here Vern sounds like Caleb, the west Texas author who described the fear instilled by fundamentalist preachers: "This, I think, is the product of our stubbornness, fear, and institutionalized ignorance brought to us by so-called conservative think-tanks that do not think, but promote fear instead and advocate only for the wealthy at the expense of the...[other classes]... They clearly intend to destroy the very thing that made us great to begin with: public education. How can we expect subsequent generations to solve increasingly complex problems when we've destroyed the mechanism by which to create the solutions? (Author's note: the children of wealth are continuing to get a good education, just not a *public* education.)

"The current political gridlock in the United States is a loud warning signal for the rest of the world, that unfettered capitalism is running amok and we are doing nothing to stop it. We cannot pray our way out of practical problems, poverty and ignorance. Beliefs don't work when actual, physical action is required. Decisions must be made to solve problems; waving incense pots and singing songs do not... [address] real, actual difficulties like starvation, constant wars and a polluted planet require real, actual actions and solutions. The energy issues, for example, already have the necessary technology to get this generation off fossil fuels. It's the gridlock of the capitalists buying governments around the world that prevents the implementation of solutions.

"We, unlike the Mayans, can see and understand what is coming, and our technology has determined how those problems can be ameliorated. *It's our will to do so that will determine whether we will once again succumb to our primitive nature of small tribe behaviors and face another collapse.* If we choose to remain in gridlock for political posturing, ideological fantasy or religious perfidy, we will most certainly face our own mortality. There are now almost eight billion of us and we are becoming increasingly interdependent. An interesting question might be: How many humans will survive the next crash and great war?"

I asked Vern how he arrived at such views, and he gave me the following information:

When he retired from twenty-two years as an industrial engineer, he taught human anatomy both at the college level and in a medical school. Subsequently, he became a public school teacher of both sciences and English. Retiring from education, he turned to writing, including books, articles, and a blog addressing politics and education.

He didn't elaborate on his family background, and I didn't pester him. We've already heard about avid learners from both education-oriented families and fundamentalist, anti-education families. We've also heard the Yeller Dawg view that here in Texas the Republicans are trying to starve the public schools. The GOP in Texas apparently fares better if their non-wealthy supporters don't know too much about science, history, or economics and aren't encouraged to ask questions. Vern does question, and he reads, and he uses reason; and though I know nothing about his finances, I know he cares about something more than getting rich. As a result of all these reasons, he isn't voting Republican in 2016.

Chapter 20: A Voice too Loud?

When Woodrow's Yeller Dawgs started meeting forty years ago, the early attendees included Nell, a woman Woodrow knew through her involvement with the Texas Board of Common Cause.[24] Nell not only served on the State Board for Common Cause, but she had run for Congress from Lubbock's 19th Congressional District, "consisting of fifteen counties, extending up the western side of the Texas Panhandle. Issues included the proposed Equal Rights Amendment, income tax rates, union membership, living conditions for farmworkers, etc."[25] She, her husband, and their two sons had moved to Austin, where she opened her own accounting practice.

Forty years later, after Donald Trump had defeated Hillary Clinton for the Presidency of the United States, I was leaving a Yeller Dawgs meeting and asked Nell for her explanation of Clinton's loss.

"Misogyny," she answered.

Given Nell's life story, that answer made sense:

Nell's grandparents, Pumphrey and Nettie arrived in Greer County in a covered wagon before the turn of the century. Their eighth child, Virginia, was born in 1910 and graduated from the University of Oklahoma at 19, marrying Ronald on graduation day. Born in 1940, Nell was their third child and only daughter.

Nell described Amarillo as "an easy place to grow up. From our home on Van Buren Street, I was able to get around town at an early age. Most days, I walked home from Wolflin School with friend and neighbor, Joe. We could cut through the Amarillo College campus, and later our route took us through the brand-new Memorial Park and straight down scenic Hughes Street, with its big ol'

---

[24] Common Cause describes itself as "the citizens' lobby, working in Washington, D.C. and state capitols for the open, honest, accountable government..."

[25] In its history Texas has sent seven women to Congress, none of them from Lubbock.

houses. My friend Penny lived in one of those houses; and when her mother wasn't home, we could slide down the bannister."

There were limits to what little girls could do, but she didn't always agree with them or follow them: "At Wolflin Elementary, I was known for being too loud in the hallways." Nevertheless, they saw leadership potential and trustworthiness in this girl; and in fourth grade, they made her a crossing guard. "I was given a cross-strap and badge to wear for a little while as the crossing guard who shepherded fellow students across the street to the little store where one could buy a hotdog and a coke with their 25-cent lunch money."

At this point, she had few complaints about a girl's life. "School was always a pleasure. We had a big playground with swings and slides, and a wonderful contraption that led to dreams of flying!" This playground contraption was eventually "deemed too dangerous" for either the boys or the girls.

Nell played softball in Physical Education. It made no difference to her that on the baseball diamonds across the street, girls played softball, while boys played baseball. She just wanted to play, and she liked being the one who did the pitching.

Growing up in Amarillo, no one thought that the absence of an organized team for girls was evidence of misogyny. Nell's father offered to coach a girl's softball team, but none of the other girls' parents showed any interest. If they had formed one team, they wouldn't have had anyone against whom they could to play anyway.

The only extracurricular activity specifically for girls was Girl Scouts, so Nell's parents joined a tennis club where she could take lessons and play. Her parents weren't discouraging her from pursuing her interests and developing her abilities.

Girls were also permitted on the student council; and Nell must have reached a leadership position because she was one of three delegates from her school to attend a national student council conference in Washington D.C. There she reports having contracted Potomac Fever, an infectious interest in politics.

When her mother, Virginia, was attending college, a young woman with such a bright mind might have been discouraged from studying math and science, but Nell took all of the high school math and physics that were offered. Since she was an excellent student, served on the student council, and scored very high on standardized tests, she applied to attend Mary Baldwin College where a cousin had studied. They took one look at her grades and test scores; and, naturally, she was admitted.

A private school degree didn't cost $100,000 in 1958, but it would have been beyond her parents' means were it not for the fact that a Mary Baldwin alumna from Detroit had funded a scholarship designated for young women from Texas. Nell won the scholarship; but because it didn't pay for transportation to and from school, she stayed in Staunton (Virginia) year-round except for Christmas and summer breaks, which she spent back home in Texas.

During one spring break she stayed with the professor who made up the entire Mathematics and Physics departments. Nell majored in math and took all the college's physics courses too. She like physics "because it explained how things worked and it was mathematical in a sense," as opposed to Chemistry which involved a whole periodic table of elements that reacted with one another in often unpredictable ways. To graduate with a major in math and a physics minor, a chemistry professor designed a Physical Chemistry course so she'd have enough physics-related courses to graduate after three years of study with a minor in physics.

While studying in Virginia, Nell was also corresponding with a young man, Paul, she'd met at the Amarillo Country Club, a golfer, not a tennis player. After graduation, they married and set up housekeeping in Lubbock while Paul finished college. Nell taught junior-high math and took enough math courses for an MA in Mathematics. During this period while she was the breadwinner, she requested "a three-month payout on a new refrigerator, and they asked her to bring Paul in to sign the loan." They wanted to say "To hell with you," but they needed the refrigerator.

While Paul was in school, one of his professors required him "to subscribe to the nascent *Texas Observer*, and that was the beginning of a whole new chapter. It was in the *Observer* that I saw a small ad saying 'Join Common Cause....the Citizens' Lobby.' The ad said 'Even you can make a difference.' Their issues included women's rights and making government more answerable to the people, so we became charter members, and I twice served as the Texas Chair of Common Cause, which involved quarterly trips to Austin for board meetings and some lobbying. Then I won the election to be a member of the CC National Governing Board and served two terms. That position took me back to DC for quarterly board meetings, chaired first by John Gardner, and then by esteemed Harvard professor, Archibald Cox. Texas Common Cause recently gave me a nice plaque honoring my two terms as state chair."

Though she was being recognized for her political work by the folks in Democratic Austin, for the first time in an academic setting, her talents as a mathematician received little appreciation:

"After Paul's graduation, we moved back to Amarillo where we had two fine sons and Paul worked as an accountant. Then I went back to Texas Tech to work on my Ph.D. in Mathematics, though I didn't finish that degree." Apparently, they didn't seem to value her as a promising math student: "As I look back, I... [feel] a little bitter that the graduate faculty never recognized my 99th - percentile score on the GRE. Oh well, I was just a girl." Then she adds, "nor did I give myself the proper respect..."

Nell left the program; and after passing the CPA exam and practicing accounting for a couple of years, she joined the Lubbock Chamber of Commerce. How did the males on the Chamber react to a woman's presence? "Nobody would even sit next to me," she said.

Then, when she and Paul joined the Country Club, it "didn't go over well" that she and her husband asked that the membership be put in her name. "Only the bartender treated me with respect. He was black, so he knew about discrimination of different kinds."

Nell didn't give up challenging west Texas' conservatism: "As a result of those Common Cause trips to Washington, I caught Potomac fever and decided to run for Congress in 1986. We were living in Lubbock at the time, and the 19th Congressional District consisted of fifteen counties, running up the western side of the Texas Panhandle. Issues included the proposed Equal Rights Amendment, income tax rates, union membership, living conditions for farmworkers, etc.

I was defeated in the Democratic primary by a Hereford farmer who had led a tractorcade to DC protesting the low prices of farm products. It didn't help that a lot of my potential supporters were drawn to the Republican primary by a former Democrat who was running for Governor... Anyway, Paul and I decided to put

Lubbock in our rear-view mirrors, and we happily moved to Austin to join our sons.

"In Austin, Paul took a job with The Texas Department of Insurance, and ended up as Associate Commissioner. I started my own accounting practice, and reunited with old friends from my years on the Common Cause State Board. The best of those friends was Woodrow. He and his wife put together a little discussion group of their Democrat friends......which was to become the Yeller Dawgs! Early members included Mack and his wife."

Forty more years pass, and only the voters of 2016 can say what they didn't like about Hillary Clinton; but to Nell, it felt personal. When she was a talented little girl, Amarillo's adults complained about her exuberant voice in the school's hallways. Much later, male academics at Texas Tech didn't appreciate her talents as a mathematician. Country Club members didn't mind her presence as a spouse but didn't want to see her as an equal, a member in her own right. Not raised to feel less than a man, perhaps such behavior felt like misogyny, as though they didn't like *her*. Did they not like her because she was female or because she aspired to be recognized as legally and intellectually equal to a man? To the woman, what difference did it make?: When she tried to be everything she could be, they didn't like it. In retrospect, she allows that "Texas may have always been slightly less misogynist than some states since it required all hands of either gender to tame the place!"

Why couldn't Nell vote Republican in 2016? One reason is clear: Because the Republicans did not have, and never have had, a female candidate for President. When she did line up to vote, the woman behind her "was practically hogtied by her husband." He scowled when Nell told her, "It will be fun to vote for a woman for president," and the woman winced. She was sure he hovered enough to prevent her from voting for the woman, maybe even "pulled the lever for her."

Among these conservative West Texans, what was missing in their response to the interests and aspirations of Nell and exceptional girls like her? Her answer rang loud and clear: *respect*.

Chapter 21: The Meeting

I'd always taken notes at meetings, though this would be the last time I did. Super Tuesday had just come and gone, and Trump and Clinton were leading in delegates. Mack was back from quadruple bypass surgery and pacemaker installation and looked fit and ready to go. Woodrow wasn't feeling well, though. We had no speaker and no candidates making pitches, so a rare free-for-all filled the meeting time.

First, the topic of education arose, and the first contribution that made it into my notes came from JW, who announced that only 39% of community college entrants finish any program within six years. I knew JW now, knew how much he had sacrificed for his own education and those of his family members, his entire career then devoted to educating others. He cited statistics showing that the Republican-controlled legislature is gutting education.

When he finished, someone respectfully reminded him, "You're preaching to the choir. It serves Republican interests to dumb down the electorate. They can't form a big enough coalition of one-percenters. They have more luck selling their fear mongering and denial of global warming to an uneducated voter. If you can keep slavery out of the American History curriculum, you can support white supremacists pretending not to be racist. If you can keep evolution out of the curriculum or discredit the science upon which it's based, you can reduce trust in the scientific methods that warn us of global warming. If you can make the voter afraid of Washington, you can bring on those opposed to any further regulation of guns. If students aren't taught about the causes of the Great Depression, they will think that the best economy is the unregulated economy.

Someone argued that another contributor to the dumbing down of America, unfortunately, is the internet. Since 2007, he reported, the U.S. has gone from 55,000 journalists to 3200. Cole, for one, sorely missed the "voices of reason" (Huntley, Brinkley, Cronkite and, later, Rather) that were at one time broadcast by network news shows.

Another Dawg then reminded us that in 1935 as Hitler was rising, Sinclair Lewis wrote the satirical novel, "It Can't Happen Here." The internet now shows pictures of Trump assuming Hitleresque poses and suggesting fascist-like policies. Few faces around the table showed any optimism.

In this knowledgeable group, someone cited the statistic that while there has been a 10% decline in income among those with no more than a high school diploma, those with advanced degrees are making 15% more than in the past. For some reason, poorly educated people with low incomes don't favor raising taxes on the very rich to finance improved education, at least not in red states. Maybe it's no coincidence that not many Republican donors support such a strategy.

As that thought was crossing my mind, Cole said. "Let's get big money out of politics. Money is power."

I wondered, *What wouldn't a Republican donor want a blue-collar red-state voter to learn in school?* Just then a journalist cited this fact: "A ninety per cent tax rate at the upper income bracket didn't depress the economy. It stimulated the economy by encouraging reinvestment, rather than profit-taking, and it financed our current highway system."

I think one of the Dawgs was quoting a FaceBook post when she asked, "Why is it so hard for the GOP party to work for all human beings, everybody,... our country. Why is that so hard?"

I puzzled, *The typical business owner wants to make a profit. The development of the nation isn't his or her priority.* And then: *Does a Republican donor want the voter pondering this?*

My Yeller Dawgs are a democratic, common-man-respecting group; and probably most of them once thought that education would lead to an electorate that could better understand complexity. One of them expressed the hope that the lack of civility would hurt the Republican candidates with the voters: "People are smarter than that," she asserted.

At that point, someone paraphrased, "No one ever went broke underestimating the intelligence of the American voter."

"Their lack of civility predicts Republican foreign policy," one asserted. "Fear mongering distracts the voter from real issues, like polluting Flint, Michigan's water supply."

A newspaper editor cited Noam Chomsky: "Chomsky says that Trump wins because the poorly educated white males are falling below expectations faster than anyone else, and they fear they are losing power. Any sense of hope is fading. With the underlying racism, he says it's reminiscent of the rise of Fascism in Europe during the last century."

Meanwhile, I wondered, *With factory jobs exported to Asian and Mexico, and low-paying manual labor going more and more to illegal immigrants, how can the unskilled, poorly educated American earn a living? Can everyone be educated into highly skilled jobs as Bill Clinton argued, or must the minimum wage go up if the unskilled are to earn a decent living?*

Meanwhile, beside me my Brazilian, non-voting wife was scribbling, "A government based on concentrating money in the hands of a few cannot be good. To prevent a wider distribution of wealth and power, it will keep the people uneducated and afraid. Uninformed, frightened people who have no ability to reason are easier to control."

With the utmost respect, I thought, *From the mouths of babes. I am fairly certain that a Republican donor doesn't want a voter going down that path.*

Chapter 22: Grandmother and Granddaughter Dawgs

Question: "Why wouldn't you two vote republican?"

(Grandmother) Flo : "I've never voted for a Republican. Actually, I used to consider it. I considered voting for Rockefeller once, but he was socially liberal and not so different from a Democrat. We're so polarized now. I could never consider voting for one now. Do you think Trump can win? What could he accomplish if he got elected? *Could* he get elected? The polls used to show he couldn't beat Hillary, but now it's not so clear. I believe that it's cynical for them to run now, knowing that the electorate is uninformed and they can lie to the voters."

Question: "According to a FaceBook post, a much younger Trump said something like, 'If I ever run for President, I'll run as a Republican. Republicans voters are so stupid, they'll believe anything."

Flo: "I don't think Republicans are curious. They are more subservient to authority. They believe what they're told and ...don't question... They love being scared, ...love seeing boogey men, and...blaming others."

Question: "This book will have footnotes directing readers to research on personality differences that support that you just said. They've found neurochemical and genetic differences between Republicans and Democrats."

Phyllis (the Grand-daughter): "The Republicans keep people who would vote against them from voting against them."

Question: "One of the Dawgs explained how that works in Dixie."

Flo: "Sometimes Republicans vote against their own best interests. Some red (Republican) states that are against big government have the most government aid. They are against aid going to some Black mother on welfare, but they receive so much aid, themselves. I don't understand it.

"And some Republicans are just protecting their own financial interests...

"Donald Trump could never be President of the United States. Do you think he cares about any of this? I don't think he can get the independents. He can't get something done just because he says he will. Furthermore, Trump is repulsive."

Question: "Instead of asking people why they can't vote Republican, I should ask them who makes them throw up."

Flo: "The worst one of all is Cruz. To me it is so obvious he's disingenuous, just plain evil... And poor Jeb Bush." (This interview took place before the South Carolina primary.)

Question: "Trump said Jeb was supposed to be the smart Bush. I think he might be smarter than George, but I'd bet George was the alpha."

Flo: "Think how many thousands of people are dead because of George (Bush)."

Question: "So, you never voted for Republican?"

Flo: "Not that I remember."

Question: "Which Republican candidate might you consider?"

Flo: "Kasich. He's actually done something--balanced budgets, allowed Obamacare in Ohio. He'd have a chance of getting independents, which is me, even though I never voted for a Republican."

Question: "How about Rubio? What's driving him?"

Flo: "Ambition. He's too immature. It's not his time. It may never be his time. He fervently researches, then spills it out as a practiced performance. He's too uncomfortable, hasn't accomplished anything in the Senate. He embraced immigration and then dumped it.

"There have to be people who are better [candidates]. We're going to have Democratic president and a Republican congress again. The most important thing about electing a Democrat is the Supreme Court nominations.

"I love Bernie Sanders. I don't care if he can't get anything done. He's wise, honorable, kind, authentic. Ted Cruz can't win against Bernie Sanders."

Phyllis: "It's dangerous to put Hillary as the nominee because it will draw out Clinton haters. Vets hate Hillary because of Benghazi. They call her a murderer."

Flo: "Here's an example of how dumb the Republicans are: They are complaining about health insurance rates going up. Well, duh, you left the insurance companies in charge of rates, so of course the rates are going to go up."

Question: "In a single payer, there are no insurance companies involved."

Flo: "It's time to start fighting for it."

After reading a verbatim, unedited account of our conversation, Flo said, "I sound like an idiot! You tricked me!"

Then I edited the transcript, and she thanked me for making her sound more reasonable. The bottom line, she said, "I cannot support any Republicans at this time because they are icky."

Political scientists don't recognize the term, *icky*. Genetically, it derives from a hybridization of concepts more from Irish (from Flo's grandfather) than German (from Flo's grandmother). Flo started hearing the term around the house during the 1960 election, which divided her parents. Her mother liked the clever Democrat, not the *icky* weirdo running as a Republican. The term describes her own mother's reaction to social injustice and her sympathy for the underdog regardless of skin color, social class, or nationality:

When Flo was still a girl, she observed the opposite of *ickiness* when a poor German immigrant woman came to clean her house that didn't really need cleaning, when a brand new vacuum cleaner was bought from the cleaning lady's struggling salesman-husband, when an unemployed African-American man with epilepsy came to do yard work, when a destitute White woman with too many children arrived with laundry to put in the family washer and dryer. In time Flow began to regard selfish, unsympathetic people as *icky*.

Icky could have been the Yeller Dawgs' final word, but another word crept in, one that encompassed ickiness and helped to explain it.

Chapter 23: The Last Word

Cole stepped in to moderate the Dawgs' meetings in Mack's absence. He was born in Texas after World War II. He was sketchy about his family of origin but didn't criticize its values or teachings except to say they were "puritanical about sex." Almost everybody was back then. That was before birth control pills.

In an email he later explained his problem with Republicanism: "My take on why rational people can't and shouldn't vote for any Republican for any office includes the basic core setup of Republicanism. Today's Republican operating system combines the worst of all worlds economically. By that I mean that they want to have little or no restrictions on anything having to do with money manipulation, profits for corporations and downward pressure on wages and workers' rights. Their fantasy of free-market enterprise being able to solve all problems has been disproven over and over, the last major event being our own Great Depression of 1929. (Author's note: Experience has shown that in markets which are free of external, government policing, sellers inflate prices to increase profits.)

"Combine the above basic philosophy with that of Milton Friedman and the Chicago Boys' economic system of *Supply-Side Economics* (aka "trickle-down" or "Reaganomics") and you have the catastrophe predicted by Karl Marx. Reaganomics is *still* the mantra of the GOP and it continues to fail the American middle class. Every time the Republican Party has gotten control over our national economics, they've created a depression, a recession, or a war. In 1932, Franklin Roosevelt implemented the elements of Keynesian economics that tells governments to get the money moving by priming the pump with capital when an economy is struggling. In other words, tax the rich and put that money to work creating jobs, which in turn, creates taxpayers. On the other hand, the Republican philosophy of "starving the beast" (i.e., the government) is the most short-sighted strategy possible and serves only the rich. The irony here is that when the middle and consumer classes have... no means to consume, the whole economy dissolves into chaos and failure.

"Dismantling government services is the biggest lie of all. Republicans want to end public education, for example, and that means only the elite will get educated. We managed to become the greatest economy and most innovative nation in the world precisely because we educated our masses *for free*. The G.I. Bill was another of those services that served up an entire generation of educated innovators, which allowed us to lead the world in everything, defeat communism, and put men on the moon. Now why would anyone want to stop doing those things that made us great, rich, and comfortable?

(Author's note: The question is rhetorical. Cole gives his answer below.)

"The Republican Party has *no* plan that creates jobs, health care for all, respect for a woman's reproductive rights, educating the poor, or dealing with the looming global problems associated with climate change. They are only about money. Their money meme is disguised with racial dog-whistles, self-righteous Constitutional interpretations, and a fantasy about having the rich rule the country by fiat rather than by governance."

I asked what he had experienced in life to bring him to such positions. Quickly summarizing his life to arrive at his answer to my question, he told of being the class clown in high school. Still, he managed to gain entrance into the University of Texas and moved from San Antonio to Austin. Not yet serious about his studies, his career, or maybe even his survival during the VietNam era, Cole "flunked out of college and into the army." Before enlistment, he had greatly admired a mentor who was an architect; and after his military service, he followed this man's footsteps into architecture school. Then came a marriage, a divorce, continued child-rearing, a career in architecture, including a tenure in the construction business.

Cole explained that despite his stint in the construction business, he loved the *art* of architecture, which showed, he said, "how I see life." Rather than reprint his portfolio, I will editorialize about the relationship between his free spirit and the things he finds meaningful about his life:

Cole didn't enter architecture to make a fortune. Though he made enough money to retire, the *business* of building didn't capture his heart. He is moved by the beauty of art, but this doesn't mean things have to be visually pretty to interest him. Art conveys a truth and arouses a feeling of insight and understanding.

So, this is a man who wants to understand and to capture and communicate his understanding in a way that others can know--know in a way that combines intellect and emotion. For example, Cole forwarded his feller Yeller Dawgs a FaceBook post with the haunting visage of James Baldwin and the following statement:

"Well, if one really wishes to know how justice is administered in a country, one does not question judges, or the protected members of the middle class, One goes to the unprotected--those, precisely, who need the law's protection most!--and listens to their testimony. Ask any Mexican, any Puerto Rican, any black man, any poor person--ask the wretched how they fare in the halls of justice, and then you will know, not whether or not the country is just, but whether or not it has any love for justice, or any concept of it. It is certain, in any case, that ignorance, allied with power, is the most ferocious enemy justice can have."

Cole hears what the wretched say, and he cares about their viewpoint. His politics "comes from a view of how humans... should relate to each other." So, when asked why he can't support a party that seems unconcerned about suffering due to poverty, or racism, or an unwanted pregnancy, or sexism, or man-made destruction of the environment, he tells this story: "When I was much younger and pondering the meaning of Evil, I kept being shunted to the Bible or other religions. To me, that always proved to be rather unsatisfying. Then, some time back in the '70's, I was watching a movie which was set during the Nuremberg trials... One lawyer said to another, 'I think I've discovered the definition of Evil: (Here Cole offers the Yeller Dawgs' last word, the crucial ingredient missing from the personalities of candidates that Gramma Flo described as "icky...") It's the absence of Empathy."

Appendix 1: An Absentee Interview with Horton Foote, author of
"The Chase"

"I apologize for not contacting you sooner, Mr. Foote."

"Sooner? What year is it?"

"Well, Sir, I'm afraid it's 2016."

"2016! I died in 2009, for heaven's sake!"

"Yes, Sir, I plan to acknowledge that fact. I didn't see your play until last year. Well, I actually didn't see your play at all. I saw the movie."

"This isn't good, not good at all."

"I'm sorry, it's just---"

"Don't interrupt! I don't care about the play any more. I don't even care that Hellman botched the screenplay. It's just sad to hear that the story is still relevant in 2016. I guess I shouldn't be surprised. The South never changes."

"I do live in Texas, Sir, but I have to admit I don't really know much about the former Confederacy. I just want to be sure I understand what you are trying to say about Texas in 1952."

"The Civil Rights legislation didn't change the South, then?"

"I don't know. I just know it's solidly Republican now."

"Damn!"

"In your play, Sir, you make race kind of a side issue."

"Oh, yeah? I hate it when some pseudo intellectual analyzes literature. What was the main issue then? "

"The crux of the story seems to be about the relationship between the wealthy man at the top of the food chain and the Whites who, one way or another, work for him. Sure, Blacks have to stay in their place, and one Black man is beaten up because he gets "uppity," but the main issue is the White guys getting a good place in line below the rich White banker at the top. They focus most of their fury on the white guy who shows up 'his betters' and crowds ahead in line."

"Yeah, yeah, so what?"

"Well, I mean, you seem to suggest that slavery was all about profits in cotton production, white supremacy was preached to justify the cruelty toward

Black slaves, and racism was just a tool to gain support from poor Whites. Is that what you meant?"

"Go on with your critique. I wrote the plays. I don't explain them."

"It's as if you're saying that the lower class Southern White remains economically limited, threatened by competition from Blacks, and upholding the legacy of White Supremacy to this day, or till 1964."

"It's not very flattering when you spell it out like that."

"But is that what you meant, sir?"

"Meant?! Have you ever tried writing literature?"

"Well, yes."

"Then you should realized the stupidity of that question. You can be a student of literature, or you can be a writer. You can't be both at the same time!"

"But your play seems to say that the problems with racism and White supremacy have never been solved and might never be solved, so our country will stay forever divided!"

"Can't you let me rest in peace?! Answer your own question. Is the South, or wherever a majority of racists live, any different in its attitudes that it was in 1865? How many White Southerners have stepped forward and said, ' We were dead wrong. What were we thinking?'"

"Then I shouldn't hold my breath waiting for a group of Whites to help pull down the Confederate flag from statehouses or remove statues of Confederate soldiers from the grounds of Austin's capital?"

Silence.

"How long does this have to go on?"

Silence

"Horton!"

Silence

Appendix 2
The Other Side of the Coin

On the other side of the political coin one finds the face of the non-Yeller Dawg. What do we see on this face? We find one or more of the following:

1. Faith in Unfettered Capitalism: Beginning with Woodrow, Cal, and Mack, the Yeller Dawgs have taught that unfettered capitalism is not the same as free enterprise. The non-Yeller Dawgs might trust that market will always have a product to solve the problem, or that the consumers will always have the wisdom to avoid dangerous products. On the other hand, the Yeller Dawg does not believe that unregulated markets will necessarily provide what is best for us in the long run. The Yeller Dawg will not support those politicians who would even do away with the Food and Drug Administration, as if the market can or did protect people from snake oil salesmen. History has shown that markets can't protect us against price-fixing or snake oil salesmen, so a politician who doesn't want to outlaw snake oil salesmen *is* a snake oil salesman, himself. Such politicians either have great faith in the common wisdom, or they are only interested in getting rich. They are not Yeller Dawgs.

2. Sanctity of Wealth. Some non-Yeller Dawgs believe that a person should have the right to keep almost all of his wealth, regardless of the needs of the nation and citizenry as a whole. The creators of the current Republican coalition are simply pursuing a goal frequently sought by the Republican Party, as stated by President Calvin Coolidge: "The business of America is business."[26] Yeller Dawgs are not likely to share the view that a large income necessarily signifies a valuable contribution to society or reflects hard work. They are more likely to see the top 1% as similar the nineteenth century Robber Barons, especially if this wealth is gained by underpaying employees. Those who believe that the great wealth of those who participate in the U.S. economy should not be taxed to maintain and improve the country in ways that individuals cannot, e.g., roads, schools, military, courts, FBI, CIA, etc., are not Yeller Dawgs.

---

[26] Yes, Lincoln was a Republican, but he departed from this central tenet when he elevated abolition of slavery above the prosperity of cotton farmers.

3. Christian Fundamentalism. Some, though certainly not all, Republicans believe in the literal correctness of Judeo-Christian scripture even if, as the Creationism Museum in Kentucky says, "human reason" tells them otherwise. The fundamentalist must reject the findings of scientific experimentation and theorizing if it violates what they are told about man's place on the planet. The Yeller Dawg is more likely to gather scientific information, rely on reason, and employ logic.

4. The Supremacy of the White European. Racists do not approve of the government's taking any action to assist people of color from rising socially, educationally, and financially because, in their view, people of color belong on the bottom. Not all Republicans hold this belief, of course, but there are people who do, and none are Yeller Dawgs.

5. All problems can be solved by hard work. Unlike the Yeller Dawgs described in these pages, people who believe that all problems can be solved by hard work do not want the government to spend any of their money (1) to provide equal opportunity or (2) ongoing help to those who are mentally or physically handicapped. Yeller Dawgs live in a community and have empathy for the suffering of others.

6. Lack of compassion for people who are different. If someone genuinely feels badly when a different kind of person is in serious distress--a Black child who cannot afford an education, a gay man prevented from marrying the man he loves, a non-terrorist refugee seeking safety from terrorism--he will find it hard to ignore this person's pleas for help. No Yeller Dawg would have said to an advocate for Civil Rights in 1963, "Why are you stirring things up? Things are fine as they are."

7. Belief in the subservience of women. Many Republicans probably don't hold to this position, but I found no Yeller Dawg who opposed a woman's right to have equal opportunities in education and employment.

When I recited this list to one of the Yeller Dawgs, though an architect and not a neurophysiologist, Cole said, "I think some of that's hard-wired." A brief excursion into studies of the relationship between voting and neurological activity, neurochemistry, and personality led to a mountain of studies cited on the internet.[27 28 29 30 31 32 33 34 35 36 37 38] More than a few mentioned a lesser capacity for what is still the last word of this study, Empathy.

---

[27] http://www.motherjones.com/politics/2013/02/brain-difference-democrats-republicans,

[28] for demographic differences, refer to:
https://books.google.com/books?id=0jU24NgiXekC&pg=PA86&lpg=PA86&dq=what+demographic+characteristics+distinguish+Republicans+versus+Democrats?&source=bl&ots=vmpLjj7N55&sig=rp1s_ntoXNMg8K22qH7WVpIVLD4&hl=en&sa=X&ved=0CCgQ6AEwAjgKahUKEwiqgdLzjZvJAhXQmYgKHaYZD34#v=onepage&q=what%20demographic%20characteristics%20distinguish%20Republicans%20versus%20Democrats%3F&f=false,

[29] per: http://cultureofempathy.com/references/Experts/George-Lakoff.htm

[30] http://healthland.time.com/2012/04/16/human-kindness-genes-withstand-threats-and-fear/

[31] http://wonderforgood.com/fear-empathy-our-american-muslim-neighbors/

[32] http://fivethirtyeight.blogs.nytimes.com/2012/12/18/in-gun-ownership-statistics-partisan-divide-is-sharp/

[33] http://www.alternet.org/story/105089/can_you_guess_a_person's_politics_by_their_personality_psychologist_team_says_yes

[34] *Maria Luisa Tucker* / AlterNet.org, Oct 28, 2008

[35] http://www.addictinginfo.org/2013/05/09/fifteen-differences/

[36] http://thesocietypages.org/socimages/2012/09/15/religion-and-race-among-democrats-and-republicans/

[37] http://www.wsj.com/articles/whit-ayres-a-daunting-demographic-challenge-for-the-gop-in-2016-1425513162,

[38] http://www.huffingtonpost.com/eric-zuesse/gallup-poll-finds-democra_b_4683688.html